"The miracle of what happens when a seed is buried in the ground is as old as the earth, as profound as Jesus, and as fresh as a blossom. Jeff Davenport has harvested it into a book that will enlarge your soul and enrich your life. Read it and grow."
—John Ortberg, author and pastor, Menlo Church,
Menlo Park, CA

"C. S. Lewis. John Ortberg. Donald Miller. They all have the knack to sneak past the 'watchful dragons' in my head and engage me with truth in unexpected ways. I've now added Jeff Davenport to that list. Jeff has a rare gift to blend metaphor, story, and humor in a way that's both flat-out fun and not-messing-around deep at the same time. Consider yourself warned."
—Brian Wells, author of *The League and the Lantern*

"Stories bring deep concepts to life. Jeff's stories will hook you and then move you to change how you see God and what He can do in someone's life."
—Nancy Duarte, CEO and best-selling author

"Jeff Davenport is the best communicator I know. It is an honor to teach with him on a regular basis. Jeff's unique ability is making God approachable and desirable to everyone he meets. He shifts the emotions and beliefs of his listeners away from lies and toward the truth, making God irresistible in the process."
—Ron Johnson, lead pastor, Restoration Community Church,
Denver, CO

"*I Am a Field* sows handfuls of story seeds and reminds us that behind even a simple story is a truth. The American faith culture has lost the gift of story in favor of worldview rhetoric. Without story we cannot truly fathom a magnificent God and His crazy love for us. Jeff's fresh voice makes this book feel more like a cup of coffee with an old friend."
—James Anderson, CEO, The New Canaan Society

"When I was a college student, God used Jeff's unpacking of biblical metaphors to transform my relationship with Him, and my entire life since then has been shaped by Jeff's teaching and example. *I Am a Field* puts on full display Jeff's incredible gift for making the wisdom of Scripture imminently relatable (and hilarious), helping us to see God's love for us and His plan for our lives with completely fresh eyes."
—Matthew J. Thomas, DPhil, assistant professor of biblical studies,
Dominican School of Philosophy and Theology, Berkeley, CA,
instructor in theology, Regent College, Vancouver, British Columbia

"*I Am A Field* by Jeff Davenport leads you to discover a God who wants to grow big things inside of you and develop a personal relationship with you. You will enjoy Jeff's vivid imagery, humor, and tons of movie motifs and iconic quotes that bring unique insights to biblical truths."
—Jackelyn Viera Iloff, senior advisor,
Lakewood Church, Houston, TX

"When our offices were across the hall from one another, Jeff and I found ourselves postponing work and instead finding time to talk about life, God, questions, and mission. This book takes me back to those days and reminds me how insightful and passionate and funny Jeff really is. Now so many more can be a part of that conversation and glean from his walk and his experience."
—Keenan Barber, pastor, Beverly Hills Presbyterian Church,
Beverly Hills, CA

"Seldom do you find a book like *I Am a Field*: affable yet challenging, effortlessly profound, full of big laughs and deep consequences. It will delight you—and it may change your life."
—Robert Klitgaard, university professor,
Claremont Graduate University

I Am a Field

BECOMING A PLACE
WHERE GOD GROWS GREAT THINGS

JEFF DAVENPORT

Grace,

Jeff

IRON STREAM
BOOKS
An imprint of Iron Stream Media
Birmingham, Alabama

Iron Stream Books
100 Missionary Ridge
Birmingham, AL 35242
IronStreamMedia.com
An imprint of Iron Stream Media

Iron Stream Books serves its authors as they express their views, which may not express the views of the publisher.

Library of Congress Cataloging-in-Publication Data

Names: Davenport, Jeff, author.
   Title: I am a field : becoming a place where God grows great things / Jeff
   Davenport.
Description: Birmingham : Iron Stream Books, 2019.
Identifiers: LCCN 2019022588 (print) | LCCN 2019022589 (ebook) | ISBN
   9781563092817 (trade paperback) | ISBN 9781563092831 (ebook)
Subjects: LCSH: Christian life. | Agriculture--Religious
   aspects--Christianity | Metaphor in the Bible. | Bible. Corinthians,
   1st, III, 9--Criticism, interpretation, etc.
Classification: LCC BV4509.5 .D2498 2019 (print) | LCC BV4509.5 (ebook) |
   DDC 248.4--dc23
LC record available at https://lccn.loc.gov/2019022588
LC ebook record available at https://lccn.loc.gov/2019022589

ISBN-13: 978-1-56309-281-7
Ebook ISBN: 978-1-56309-283-1

1 2 3 4 5—23 22 21 20 19

To Mom and Dad . . . for always believing the best about me, even though I often disagreed. I'm really proud to be your son.

To Kristin . . . for being so relentless in your encouragement that I couldn't help but keep going. I love you!

To the family and friends mentioned inside . . . for co-laboring with God—planting seeds, watering them, and helping good things grow in me. Thank you for your unique and invaluable contributions.

To Bob . . . for pulling me aside years ago and telling me to write a book . . . and for years later guiding me through the process as the wise friend you are. No Bob, no book.

For Charlotte Mae and Juliette . . . so you'll always know how your daddy thinks about God.

Contents

The Field and the Farmer

Picture a field.

Vast acres of wide open, untouched land.

It's mostly dirt. Dry, dusty, seemingly uninteresting dirt.

Rocks litter the land. Some of the rocks are small and baseball-sized with an inch or two jutting up out of the ground. Other rocks are boulders weighing hundreds of pounds, sticking far enough up so they can be seen from a quarter-mile away.

A massive briar patch lies on the west end of the field. The tangle of prickly, wiry shrubs is so thick you can hardly see into it. Covering at least an acre, the briar patch feels like nature's way of saying, "No trespassing. Keep out. Stay away."

A few trees dot the field, but they're not much to look at. Some are so rotted by pine beetles it seems as though a stiff wind could blow them to splinters and dust. Others may be fruit trees, but they clearly haven't shown bud in a long, long time. Stumps pockmark the land too. With roots that dive deep into the ground, these stumps serve as stubborn tombstones—reminders of once mighty trees now fallen by lightning strike or beaver teeth.

And then there are the weeds. Almost every variety of weed— wild plants that serve no purpose except to choke out any plant that might exist for a greater purpose—has made its way up from the dirt all across the field. Kudzu, hemlock, buffalo bur, and shepherd's purse rise up, gnarly and defiant from the dry ground. "This land is ours," the weeds seem to growl.

There are a few signs of productive life on the field, though: A small patch of pale green grass that has somehow sprung up just outside the shadow of one of the larger rocks. An old apple tree on the southern edge of the field has a few shriveled, barely red pippins hanging off it. Near the briar patch bramble, there's even a tiny rose bush with a solitary pink bud considering whether or not to ever open.

On the southwest edge stands an old farmhouse and a red barn that are a sparrow's sneeze away from collapsing.

Passersby show no interest in this field. Who can blame them?

The field is largely unproductive.

It appears to have no promise.

It's more dead than alive.

That's the field.

Now, picture a Farmer.

This Farmer ambles along in his held-together-with-prayer-and-chicken-coop-wire pickup truck on the road bordering the field.

Suddenly, he stops the truck.

He climbs out, crosses the street, and walks up to the field.

This Farmer is tall and broad and tough.

He wears a green and yellow John Deere cap that's seen better years. A checked flannel button-down peeks out from beneath a dust-caked pair of brown Carhartt overalls. On his feet are a pair of Red Wing ropers so weathered they look as though they were born underground.

His face is creased and folded from years in the sun. His rough hands look to be made of hundred-year-old baseball mitt leather. His wide shoulders would have no problem swinging an axe for hours without a break. And the grit in his eyes tells you he's so flinty and strong he could use barbed wire as shoelaces if the need arose.

Those eyes are also clear, focused, and somehow kind as well. There's a light in them. A hope. An optimism. A "Sure, it'll take some work, but let's do this" attitude.

With a hand shielding those eyes from the glaring sun, the Farmer takes a good, hard look at the field.

He sees the dirt and the rocks and the dying trees and the briar patch and the stumps and the weeds.

But he seems to see something else too.

What he sees isn't apparent.

He walks the field, taking in every acre, and with every step, a smile spreads across his face.

An hour later, this Farmer makes his way back to his pickup truck.

With a nod and that grin, he fires up the engine.

And he drives into town—

—directly to the courthouse to ask the land and title clerk about the field.

After that, he hurries to the bank. Striding through the door, he heads straight for a banker, and holding a scrap of paper with the location of the land on it, he says, "I want to buy this field." He pauses and stares into the banker's eyes. "No matter the cost."

By week's end, the field is owned by the man in the John Deere cap and dirty overalls.

And it's all done with the excitement and joy of a child on Christmas Eve.

That is the Farmer.

Knowing the Unknown

THE MAP IN MY OFFICE

I have a map of Iceland hanging in my office. The shape of Iceland isn't immediately recognizable—it looks like someone threw a snowball at a wall from a moving car, then drew a line around the splat—so people often ask about it when they stop by. I tell them how I've been fascinated by arctic lands since I was in high school, have always wanted to visit somewhere like Iceland, Greenland, or the Faroe Islands, and was finally able to stop by Iceland for a few days on the way home from an overseas trip a few years back.

Then something interesting happens. No matter who they are, every person responds in the same way, asking the exact same question, word-for-word:

"What's Iceland like?"

Now, they could've expressed their curiosity about that mysterious land by saying, "Tell me about Iceland." But they don't. Instead, they ask, "What's Iceland like?"

"What's it like?" is the basis of a question we ask twenty times a day, isn't it?

"What does your new car look like?"

"What's this 'pumpkin ravioli' on the menu taste like?

"Really? Another new boyfriend? Well, what's *this* one like?"

We ask "What's (something) like?" because something inside of us knows that to understand something unknown—

—a new car—

—the pumpkin ravioli—

—a replacement boyfriend—

—it helps to have it compared to something we already know. "My new car looks just like Tory's, except it's blue." "It's like pieces of pasta giving hugs to tiny pumpkin pies." "You know how you're real judge-y? He's not like that. At all."

So, when people ask me, "What's Iceland like?" I respond with:

"Iceland is like the moon."

I say this because, though no one who's ever been in my office has visited the moon (unless I've entertained Apollo astronauts unaware), everyone has some knowledge of the moon. From NASA footage and photographs, they know the moon is barren, stark, rocky, and lonely. They also know it's strangely mysterious and oddly alluring. (If they're lunar junkies, like me, Buzz Aldrin's apropos description, "magnificent desolation," may come to mind).

I add: "You know how on the moon it looks like there's nothing for miles except rocks? There are rock fields in Iceland that seem to go on forever like that."

But that's not a nearly complete picture of Iceland. So I add: "If you've been to Europe, visiting Iceland is like visiting another unusual, intriguing European city. A confusing language, colorful street signs, interesting but reserved people."

Then I might pile on a bit more with: "Visiting Iceland is like going to a really great art museum that has so much amazing stuff that every time you turn a corner, your breath is taken away, and all you want to do is keep seeing new things because the beauty's so unusual and amazing. But instead of paintings, you're looking at massive waterfalls, towering geysers, and ten-mile wide glaciers."

Their original question could be reworded this way: "I don't know much about Iceland, so what can you compare it to so I can better understand it?"

Or, put another way, they're asking me to use the known to explain the unknown.

METAPHORS, METAPHORS EVERYWHERE

If I were your fourth grade grammar teacher, Mrs. McGillicutty, I'd tell you a metaphor is a figure of speech wherein one object or idea is applied to an object or action to which it is not literally applicable. But, since I'm not Mrs. McGillicutty, I get to provide my own definition and, for the purposes of this book, it will be: a metaphor is something that uses the known to define the unknown.

When you think of them in such simple terms, it's easier to see that metaphors are all around us.

Shakespeare tells us, "All the world's a stage," (*As You Like It*) to communicate the importance of every person stepping up and playing their part at the right time. Life isn't, obviously, a stage. But it's kind of like one.

When Gerald Ford became president following the resignation of Richard Nixon, he told the American people, "Our long, national nightmare is over." Now, it wasn't like every person in the United States was asleep and sharing the same awful dream. No. But his language put words to what a lot of people were feeling: "This Watergate thing was an intense, stressful time—like a nightmare—that we all experienced together. Thankfully, it's over."

The Beatles want us to know their current exhaustion levels, so they compare their work ethic to that of a dog. (Because, of course, when you think of a hard-working animal, you think of a golden retriever.) Also, they tell us they should be resting like a thick tree branch.

My buddy's Texas dad calls intense rainstorms "frog stranglers" to give a sense of how hard it's raining—and because he's a pretty funny guy.

The stories that surround us can also serve as powerful, extended metaphors, whether they're found in books, TV shows, or movies.

When I saw *The Matrix* for the first time, I liked all the crazy kung fu and special effects, but what really grabbed me was how Neo's story reminded me of my own. Not because I can dodge bullets or bend spoons with my brain, but because, like Neo, I've discovered there's a world beyond the world I can see with my eyes, and there's a battle raging to rescue people I'm meant to join. A movie about martial arts and robots that turn people into batteries actually helps me better understand who I am and what I'm meant to do in the world.

The King's Speech is a great metaphor for the difficulties and challenges of finding your voice. It's an inspiring movie, but only inasmuch as you see yourself in the main character, King George. If you identify with him—not as someone with a literal speech impediment but as someone with something worth saying yet difficulty getting it out—then the movie resonates with you as it gives you a clearer picture of your fight, reasons behind your obstacles, and ways to overcome them.

Try imagining Han Solo as the main character the next time you watch *Star Wars*. As Han goes from living life alone (except for his buddy who looks like he was created from a cleaned-out hairbrush) to joining a cause alongside his friends, you see the movie as a pretty impactful metaphor about the power of friendship, the lure of selfishness, and the joy of self-sacrifice for a greater cause. When I watch it that way, I become more firmly convinced those ideals are true in real life too.

GOD LIKES METAPHORS

Let's say it's a boring Thursday night, and you decide to come up with a list of three really, really hard-to-understand concepts. If you did that, your list may look like mine:

God
Me
What God's Doing In and Around Me

Obviously that's not an exhaustive list of hard-to-understand concepts, but it's a pretty good start, right? In fact, if you really "got" those concepts, all of the other confusing ideas in the world might start to make a little more sense. (Except calculus. No one gets calculus. They just pretend they do.)

In my time on earth, I've found that though He doesn't give answers for everything, God likes shedding light on core concepts like the ones on that list. He knows it's important for us to see Him, ourselves, and all that's swirling inside of us and around us more and more clearly if we're to live the lives we're meant to live. How does God do that?

Working through a bunch of folks' hands and brains, God wrote the Bible. The Bible is full of lots (and lots and lots) of words. Those words were written to help us understand those three big concepts better.

In some places in the Bible, God comes right out and tells us things explicitly. In the first book of the Bible (Genesis), God tells us, flat-out, that He's existed since before the earth. He also says He made the world and howler monkeys and roly-polies and the first people. In other places in the Bible, He communicates pretty plainly, "Hey, these are good things for you to do while you're alive." And, in others, "Here are some things you really don't want to be doing." And He tells stories about what really happened to actual human beings as they lived their lives, interacting with God.

Do sections of the Bible like those really help us understand those hard-to-understand concepts, though? I say: yes, sure. To some degree. I mean, if the Bible just told me, "There's a God out there. And He's really big. Like, 'goes on forever and forever' big . . . and He's always existed . . . and He made the world and people out of nothing . . . and He's doing some cool stuff to make things right until the end of time," that'd get me on the right path, but it still leaves a lot out, right? It's a big-picture view, but it's still vague. It doesn't exactly make me understand or "get" those hard-to-understand concepts.

So what does God do when He's trying to communicate with someone who wants to better understand something? He compares the un-understood with something that is understood.

God uses metaphors.

Judging from how often they're used in the Bible, God loves metaphors. He loves using things us humans know to help us better understand what we don't know.

Say you were wondering what it's really meant to be like when you're excited about God and having a relationship with Him. Now, read this little verse from the Book of Psalms: "As the deer pants for streams of water, so my soul pants for you, my God" (Psalm 42:1).

We may not know much about deer and how thirsty they get, but we've seen other animals drink. Think about a dog who's been playing in the yard, chasing a stick, ball, squirrel, or combination of the three for two hours straight. Then, imagine you set out a bowl of water. That dog doesn't just drink—it laps. And it laps it up happy. It couldn't be more excited about that water. It wants that water so much it sticks its head right down in to get a drink.

The poet writing that verse is saying, "You know how animals love to drink water when they find it? They can't get enough of it? That's how my soul feels about God. I can't get enough of Him. It just makes me so happy. And like a deer needs water, my soul needs God."

Now, let's say one day you're wondering how God feels about people who've walked away from Him. Then you read this little story Jesus tells:

> Suppose a woman has ten silver coins and loses one. Doesn't she light a lamp, sweep the house and search carefully until she finds it? And when she finds it, she calls her friends and neighbors together and says, "Rejoice with me; I have found my lost coin." In the same way, I tell you, there is rejoicing in the presence of the angels of God over one sinner who repents.
>
> —Luke 15:8

This metaphor tells you God doesn't just write people off. Like an old lady who's about to lose her mind unless she finds what she's looking for, God chases people down until He finds them. And just like the old lady doesn't yell at the coin, God doesn't yell at us. And like the old lady has a party, God celebrates our return.

Here's one of the most famous metaphors in the entire Bible: "The LORD is my shepherd" (Psalm 23:1).

David, the writer of this psalm, spends the whole song (Did you know all the psalms were written to be sung?) comparing God's guidance and care to a shepherd's care for his sheep. Furthermore, to help us understand ourselves, David compares us to sheep.

In all of these metaphors, God uses known concepts (thirsty animals, someone who can't rest until they've found what they lost, shepherds and sheep) to help us understand hard-to-understand concepts (passion for God, God's forgiving nature, how God wants to guide us).

Through metaphors, God uses the *known* to define the *unknown*. They help us little humans understand a bit better the perspective of big, giant God. They're one of God's gifts to us. And me? I'm grateful for them.

THIS METAPHOR AND THIS BOOK

A few years ago, I led a program designed to help Pepperdine college students (Go Waves!) as they followed God. One Tuesday night, a few hours before I had to go out and teach a few hundred kids, I realized I had nothing to share. So I just started reading the Bible—which is, of course, a pretty good idea. I ran across a small, seemingly insignificant sentence that grabbed me right when I read it. It was a metaphor. And, in a moment, I saw so much of what that metaphor meant and how it could help us understand those three big concepts (God, Me, and What God's Doing In and Around Me) better. As I thought about it, it started to impact me, personally.

I went out and taught about it that night. A week later I found out the metaphor had a profound effect on a number of students. So I thought about it some more. Chewed on it some more. Unpacked it some more. And whenever I had an opportunity to speak to various groups, I'd teach on this metaphor. Each time it seemed to help people untangle knots, get some clarity, and help them follow and trust God a little better.

So this book is just me, taking a small, simple metaphor in the Bible, and blowing it out, diving down deep into it, and trying to communicate what I think God may be saying to us through it.

This book is also just *me*. I don't want this book to read like some heavy, super-serious Treatise on God and You and All Ye Shall Doeth Because of Such Truth. No. That's not me and, I assume, that's not you either.

I meet with a lot of people over coffee to talk with them about their lives. My goal is to listen, identify places where it seems God is moving, and encourage them to follow Him and His love for them.

My goal isn't to come across as Gandalf of the Starbucks. My goal is to come across as Jeff Davenport—a guy who's living his own life, struggling through it on some days and doing better on others, trying to figure out what God's doing in and around him too.

I hope this book reads like a coffee-shop conversation. (Though it will be, admittedly, a pretty one-sided conversation. I mean, you can talk back to this book if you want, but the odds are pretty low I'm going to hear you.) I hope this book reads like me casually telling you what I've seen—the stories I've lived and the stories I've seen others live—and some of the things I feel God's shown me through all of that. The goal is you move a little further down the road in your relationship with God. I hope you finish the book feeling more excited about your life and what God's doing in that life He's given you.

I hope God uses this book to communicate to you about the unknown things in your life by comparing them to known things.

I had a pal once tell me, with a scoff, that metaphors were just for the simpleminded. Well, I've come to happily agree with him. I agree with him mainly because I know I'm pretty simpleminded, and metaphors consistently help me understand things better.

So if you're simpleminded too—if you like and need metaphors to get a better handle on things—welcome.

Chapter 1
The End

You are God's field.

—1 Corinthians 3:9

With an early afternoon sun slapping hard on the back of his neck, the Farmer walks across the field he's purchased. As he walks, he runs a pocketknife across the end of a pencil, sharpening it bit by bit.

Every acre, the Farmer pauses, lifts his hat, wipes the sweat from his forehead with the back of his arm, and looks out at the field. He scratches the stubble on his jaw, squints an eye, and thinks.

Any bystander would wonder what in the world this farmer was doing, because who would ever think much—if anything—of this field? The rocks, the weeds, the stumps, the barrenness all scream out, "This place isn't worth the thought."

But the Farmer is, indeed, thinking about that field.

He's not just thinking, though. He's imagining. He's dreaming. He's wondering.

When a thought crosses his mind, he pulls an old envelope out of his back pocket and jots something down on the back of it with his pencil. He smiles and nods at what he's written, then puts the envelope back into his pocket and continues whittling the pencil tip as he walks farther across the field.

He pushes through thickets, steps over rocks, crosses a grove of half-burned, lightning-struck trees, and clamors up and down ditches and dry creek beds.

As the day goes on and the sun burns hotter, the Farmer's energy only increases. So does the look of wonderment on his face and the pace of his steps.

Finally, just as the sun is starting to give up and fall toward the horizon, the Farmer completes his rounds.

He marches across the field to the barn. He stops and puts the envelope up against the barn door so he can get a good look at it in the fading light.

From his scrawl, he quietly reads aloud to himself a list—

Corn
Wheat
Cotton
Potatoes
Apples
Roses—white, pink, yellow

His list goes on, and as he reads each item, he taps his pencil against the name of each crop as though to say, "Yes. Indeed."

When he's reached the end of the list, he turns back toward the field and looks out.

With his physical eyes, he doesn't see those crops. But in his mind's eye, he sees every one growing up out of rich, thick soil, bursting with flower and fruit. It's hard for the Farmer to separate out reality: what's currently out in the field from what he's envisioning.

To him, it doesn't matter though. What he sees is a beautiful sight.

It's a familiar one too. This isn't the first field the Farmer has taken on. He's done this time after time after time.

But to the Farmer, each field is entirely different.

Each has its own unique make up and challenges.

And each also has its own unique set of possibilities.

To the outsider, this field may seem like any other, untended, run-of-the-mill, plot of land.

To the Farmer, each are as singular as snowflakes.

To him, this field is different.

And it's that specialness that makes the Farmer delight in the field.

He's not just delighting in what the field could grow, though. He's just plain delighting in the field itself.

That delight is what drives him—drives him to turn the field into something more than it currently is.

It's what drives him to bring about something good.

YOU, A LONG, LONG TIME AGO

Imagine it's the year AD 50, and you live in the hustling, bustling Greek city of Corinth.

Your life is simple. You wear tunics and sandals every day. You get absolutely no cell service (which is fine because you don't have a cell phone). Dust and its removal are some of your biggest problems.

You're an average Greek person except for one thing: though you live in the land of gods like Zeus and Ares and Athena, you've come to believe in a guy named Jesus. You believe He actually lived and walked around on the earth about twenty years ago. You also believe He had a lot of great ideas about what God is like, how people should treat each other, and the best way to live. You don't just believe this guy was a great teacher, though. You believe He was the living, breathing Son of God who was killed by people who didn't like Him yet rose from the dead three days later. Wild, huh?

You believe all of this because someone came to Corinth telling people about this Jesus guy, what He taught, what He did, and how He loves everybody and wants each individual person to believe in Him, receive His love, be forgiven, and follow Him.

The person who taught you may have been a guy named Paul (who you've heard crazy stories about). Or it could've been a different fella named Apollos (which is a very cool name). Or it could've been Penelope, the kind, older lady down the street who'd received such life-altering love from Jesus she couldn't keep her newfound passion to herself. Or that one guy who has a funny-looking scar.

Initially, all of the Jesus-followers hang out together, live life together, and love each other really well.

But soon, this big, happy group starts to splinter off into factions.

One faction is made up of people who say they "belong" to Paul because Paul was the one who taught them about Jesus.

Another faction is people who say they "belong" to Apollos because he was the way they came to know Jesus.

Another is the "I belong to Penelope" faction.

And then there's the faction of people who say they "belong" to That One Guy Whose Name You Can't Quite Remember, But He Has a Scar on His Cheek That's Kind of in the Shape of a Shrimp Fork.

It's become a mess with the factions not getting along, thinking one is more right than the other.

Then a letter shows up in Corinth. It's from Paul.

After a few weeks of this letter (basically a scroll with a stamp on it) being passed around from faction to faction, it finally ends up with your group where one of your friends reads it aloud.

After some opening niceties about how thankful Paul is for all of the people who love Jesus and live in Corinth, Paul gets to the elephant in the room. Suddenly, you realize this letter isn't going to be a "Hey, buddies! How's it going? Hope you're having a rad summer!" kind of letter. Paul writes:

Are you not acting like mere humans?

(Meaning: you're behaving like regular-Joe people who don't know Jesus and don't think His thoughts on how people should interact with each other and treat each other matters. Yikes.)

For when one says, "I follow Paul," and another, "I follow Apollos," are you not mere human beings?

What, after all, is Apollos? And what is Paul? Only servants, through whom you came to believe—as the Lord has assigned to each his task. Maybe Paul planted the seed, but Apollos watered it, and it is God who has been making it grow. So neither the one who plants nor the one who waters is anything, but only God, who makes things grow.

The one who plants and the one who waters have one purpose, and they will each be rewarded according to their own labor. For we are coworkers in God's service. (See 1 Corinthians 3:3–9.)

Paul basically makes the point that no Jesus followers "belong" to anybody, except to God.

Then, to put a cap on the concept and drive it home with a metaphor, he writes:

You are God's field.

And then you realize that all of you Jesus-followers in Corinth have been acting as though the hand hired to run the field actually owns the field. That's not the case. The field belongs to God.

With that, you decide you'll do what you can to stop thinking of yourself as Paul's or Apollos's or Fork Scar's. Instead, you'll think of yourself—and all of your Jesus-following friends—as belonging to God.

But something about this metaphor grabs you. As your friend continues to read aloud, you stare out the window and think.

You imagine yourself, not as a person but as a plot of land. And you imagine that land belonging to an unseen farmer—God.

Suddenly that little metaphor has your mind running, imagining what farmers do with fields, how fields are meant to respond to the farmer, and what good could come from the work a farmer does with a field. As you think through those things, you realize this little metaphor may be helpful for understanding God better. And yourself. And the world. And what God wants to do in your life.

THE CORE QUESTION

When you first think of this metaphor, you may (like me) immediately think of a list of things a farmer does—getting up early, pulling weeds, plowing, planting seeds, spreading animal poop all over the place, chasing off crows and varmints, sweating in the baking sun, watching the skies for rain, waiting through the winter, and finally harvesting all you've grown.

Then you may consider how those actions relate to the things God does in our lives.

But before we get to what a farmer does with a field and what this means for us and our lives, it'd be helpful to ask an underlying question first.

Why?

Why does a farmer do all those things? Why does a farmer sweat and plow and wait and handle animal poo? Why does he put in the effort?

Because a farmer has a vision.

A farmer doesn't just see the weed-ridden, dry and dusty, seemingly barren land in front of him. He sees what the land can become.

A farmer sees what can be grown.

That's what makes a farmer get up early and weed and plow and plant and, eventually, harvest.

A farmer does what he does because he sees the end.

So we might ask ourselves: If God is a farmer and I am His field, then why does He do what He does with me?

Because God has a vision.

God doesn't just see our lives as they currently are. He sees what our lives can become.

God sees what can be grown in us.

That's what makes Him do all He does in us.

God does what He does because He sees the end.

I've come to truly believe this for myself. I really believe God sees me as a wonderful place where He can grow great things.

I don't just believe this about me, though. I believe this about my wife. And my daughters. And my extended family. And my friends. And strangers.

And you.

Yeah, even though I probably don't know you, I believe God sees you this way. He sees the potential, the prospects, and the promise in you. He sees you as a wonderful place where He can grow great things.

God is a farmer.

You are His field.

SAME, BUT DIFFERENT

So what is the end God has in mind for us?

Well, it's the same for every person on earth.

But it's also different for every person on earth—meaning it's unique and individual, planned specifically for us by the God who knows us best.

First, the same part.

> For those God foreknew he also predestined to be conformed to the image of his Son, that he might be the firstborn among many brothers and sisters.
>
> —Romans 8:29

That's a pretty big mouthful of theology, sure. But the part we want to grab is this: *Conformed to the image of His Son.*

It's our destiny for God to make us like Jesus.

That's the end God has in mind for me. And my wife. And my daughters. And the rest of my family. And my friends. And strangers. And you.

God, the Farmer, looks at our fields and believes they can eventually look like Jesus' field.

Jesus' field is full of wonderful things. Things like mercy and faith and miracles and wisdom and self-control and optimism and contentment and perseverance and gratefulness and the ability to teach and heal and help and a deep, permanent love for God.

Now, I don't know about you, but there's a lot about my field that looks nothing like Jesus' field. There's some good stuff like some compassion and a drive to be a good husband and a batch of kindness, but there's also stuff like me getting really, really mad at people who—even though the lane they're in is clearly about to end—dive into my lane at the last second without so much as a turn signal or a hand wave. It's also full of me wanting to spend less time looking at my Bible and more time mindlessly scrolling through Netflix options. It's chockablock with me rolling my eyes at my wife when she says something that bugs me, impatience with my girls, frustration with myself and my shortcomings, and an obsession over getting anything shiny and new and updated with a new operating system (preferably made by a company with a piece of fruit as its logo).

I don't look at my field and think, "Now that's a Jesus field!" No. I look at it and think, "That's really mostly a Jeff field. Let's not look at it too closely, okay? Thanks."

But Jesus doesn't look at my field and get all down and frustrated and embarrassed. He looks at my field and thinks, "That's okay. I can turn that into more of a Jesus field."

What? That hardly makes any sense to me.

I mean, a Jesus field is full of things like patience and kindness and lack of eye rolling, and love for strangers, and a desire to do good things that actually translates into action, and contentedness.

God wants to turn my field into a Jesus field? To that, I say, "Well, good luck, God."

(To which, I think, God says, "Hey, thanks. But I don't really need luck. I'm God, so . . . I've got this.")

Isn't that crazy? God wants to make us like Jesus. That's what He's up to, farming away on our field while we're down here on earth (and finishing it all up when we get up to heaven).

I have to confess something, though. As exciting and as cool as being made to be more and more like Jesus, The Most Perfect Guy Who Ever Lived is, when I first learned this concept, I got . . . scared.

I got scared because I was firmly convinced that what this really deep-down meant was that I—along with anyone else who God was "conforming into the image of His Son"—was going to be, basically, lobotomized. Our personalities would be removed by God. We'd all be exact copies of one another. Millions of little Jesuses walking around, each indistinguishable from the next. A Jesus clone army. Beards and white robes and blue sashes and enough patience to deal with a thousand billion clogged-by-clueless-people-who-can't-seem-to-find-the-UPC-code-on-their-gallon-of-milk grocery store self-checkout lines.

Over time, though, I've learned this isn't God's plan. Yes, God wants us all to become more and more like Jesus, but that's not the whole picture.

In the 1930s a British bandleader named Ray Noble wrote a song called "Cherokee." It's a fun, jaunty swing tune featuring a simple, upbeat melody. In 1939, Charlie Barnet and His Orchestra recorded "Cherokee," and it became a hit, reaching number fifteen on the pop charts.

The song became so popular with musicians, bandleaders, and singers that "Cherokee" has been recorded hundreds of times. Just go to YouTube and search "Cherokee jazz standard" to find a long list of entries spanning the nearly ninety years since the song was written.

But here's the thing: none of the recordings are the same. None.

Some are played fast—way faster than old man Barnet's version.

Some are played slow—turning the happy tune into something more like a dirge.

Some feature saxophones. Some feature trumpets. Some feature female singers. Some, male. A few feature vibraphones (the "vibes" is a cool, jazzy xylophone of which I'm a big fan).

There are versions by Clifford Brown and Max Roach, Donna Hightower, Art Tatum, and Buddy Rich and Lionel Hampton (King of the Vibes!).

Probably the most famous version was recorded in 1943 by Charlie "Bird" Parker, a wildly inventive Kansas City jazz saxophonist. His take on "Cherokee" is so out there—so full of crazy, inspired, out-of-nowhere improvisation—that it's become infamous in jazz history as the moment the form shifted from "playing the notes on the page" to "playing the notes between and around the notes on the page too."

One song. Hundreds of versions of it. Each one unique, played in different ways, with different featured instruments, different emphases, and different styles.

Which one is the "right" version? None of them. Or, rather, all of them.

All of the songs are the same . . . but different.

That's like us Jesus followers. We're each meant to be conformed into the image of Jesus. But that doesn't mean we lose our unique focuses, interests, and personalities. We're to become Jesus while holding onto who He specially made us to be too.

We all play "Cherokee," but we each play it in our own style.

I currently spend much of my time as an executive speaker coach. That means I travel around, working with leaders of big businesses and nonprofits to help them speak more comfortably and dynamically in front of audiences.

My goal is for them to become fantastic, incredible, persuasive presenters. I want that for all of them.

But I don't want all my clients to end up sounding the same.

I have one client who has a natural ability to tell stories with passion and emotion. Another knows how to make data come alive when she speaks. Another is just plain funny.

I want each of my clients to get better as speakers—modulating their volume, pace, and pitch; communicating trustworthiness by using open body language; owning the entire stage—but I don't want them to lose those things that make them unique. I want their personality, distinct strengths, and individual sparks to come out when they deliver a speech. Only then do they truly become fantastic, incredible, persuasive presenters.

We're all meant to be transformed more and more into Jesus—but in ways specific to us.

We're each meant to become a unique expression of Jesus.

And that variety is one of the things that makes the church—the body of Jesus believers—so beautiful.

MAE MAE, BOMBER, AND THEIR EVIL DADDY

Now's a good time to introduce you to Mae Mae and Bomber, our two daughters.

Charlotte Mae is currently six years old. She's an incredible little girl who's had my heart since the moment she was born. She's genuinely funny, remarkably smart, used to have an imaginary husband named John, always wants to wrestle me, and loves to be loving. We call her Mae Mae.

Juliette is four. Like, really, really four. She's this cute blonde bundle who's just as sweet and loving as Mae Mae, but this kid's got a fearless streak. If she wants to do something, she dives right into it. She's happy and daring and full of life and more courageous than a team of Navy SEALS. She's actually a lot like my wife Kristin. We call this kid who runs at life without reservation, "Bomber."

I love giving things to these girls. I love buying them dumb, little gifts I find in the dollar bin at the store. I love getting them books about outer space or princesses or princesses in outer space. I love getting them silly plastic elephants they can ride around the house on while the elephants beep out repeated digital songs. (These songs haunt my sleep and will eventually cause me to give the plastic elephants away.)

But I also want to give them better things than trinkets and books and musical pachyderms.

By the time the girls leave our house, I want my wife and I to have given Mae Mae and Bomber:

A long-term view: I want them to operate less out of a desire to get short-term pleasure and more out of a desire to get what's even better in the long-term.

Encouragement: I want both of my daughters to become the all-star, varsity-level encourager Kristin is. I want people to want to be around them because they feel inspired to move toward the good and away from the bad.

Security: I want Mae Mae and Bomber so secure in who they are—and who God says they are—they can face any challenge and not be deeply rattled.

That list could go on and on, but those are some pretty good gifts. If those little birdies fly off with those gifts under their wings, we'll feel like their time in the nest was a success.

I bet, right now, you're thinking what I'm thinking: that I'm one fantastic dad. That's right! I am! Yeah. And here's a Bible verse to prove it:

> If you, then, though you are evil, know how to give good gifts to your children, how much more will your Father in heaven give good gifts to those who ask him!
>
> —Matthew 7:11

Hey! Wait a minute! That doesn't say I'm a fantastic dad! It says I'm evil. C'mon, Jesus! Be a buddy!

Of course Jesus is right. Compared to God, I'm pretty evil—with plenty of not-so-good intentions in my heart. I'm a fallen human.

But this verse actually says less about me and more about God.

It says that if a dad who lives down here on earth wants to give things that are good to his kids, how much more good are the things that God—Our Great, Awesome, Totally Wonderful Father in Heaven—wants to give us?

I have to say: I'm excited about the things I want to help develop inside my daughters. But I'm doubly excited about all the great things God is going to grow inside those little girls. I'm excited to see the unique expression of Jesus God's going to create out of each of them.

Here's the thing: the stuff God wants to grow in my girls is incredibly good stuff. It's the kind of stuff my girls will come to appreciate and treasure. It's the kind of stuff they're going to want God to have grown in them. It's also the kind of stuff the people around them—their friends, their acquaintances, their husbands (wouldn't it be crazy if Mae Mae married an actual non-imaginary man named John?), strangers—will admire and love about them. It's the stuff in them that will show other people what God is kind of like.

The things God wants to grow inside of us are what we honestly, deep down want grown inside of us. We may not know what that stuff is, but something inside us knows it'll be better than what we have now.

Well, what does this look like? What *could* this look like? Again, it takes a different form in everyone, but let's consider my pal Matt.

Matt is a dentist. But he's not one of those nerdy, boring, Muzak-loving dentists who wears a white smock with buttons to the side. Matt's one of the coolest guys I know. He rides his bike to work, gets up super early to watch live European soccer matches on TV, can talk knowledgeably about almost any topic, and listens to a lot of Jay-Z.

Dr. Matt, DDS, (as I like to call him) came out of dental school a few years ago at the top of his class. This dude could've gone off and made a million bucks hanging out a shingle in the suburbs of Denver, whitening soccer mom teeth, putting braces on kids whose teeth are only 98 percent perfectly aligned already, or filling cavities in Broncos who can't be bothered to floss. Instead, right after graduating, Dr. Matt, DDS, took a job with a nonprofit that provides healthcare for under-resourced patients.

Dr. Matt, DDS, became a dentist for poor people.

That means Dr. Matt, DDS, spends his days with his hands inside the mouths of people who don't own toothbrushes. And addicts who've used so much meth their teeth are literally rotting out. Or kids with such rampant dental problems due to neglect there's concern their adult teeth won't come in right.

A lot of these people don't speak English. So whereas my Spanish is limited to words like *manzana* and *rojo* and *hola*, Dr. Matt, DDS's, includes the Spanish words for "dental bridge," "periodontal erosion," and "oropharyngeal cancer."

Not exactly glamorous work.

To boot, Dr. Matt, DDS, gets paid a fraction of what he'd get working for regular Joe folk who brush after every meal and get check-ups twice a year.

Here's the thing: Dr. Matt, DDS, loves his job. He's not whining and complaining about getting paid less to do challenging dental work with non-English speakers. He loves it. He's been working there six years and is now actually running the place.

So how does a guy who grew up in a wealthy area of Arizona, attended a posh school like Pepperdine University, aced dental school, and had every opportunity in the world to cash in on his talents make the choice to accept a job like this?

I think it's because God had a vision in mind for Matt and his life. I think it's because God the Farmer looked at Matt and thought, "I'm going to grow good things in that guy. Things like selflessness. And empathy. And generosity. And joy in hard work. And . . . goodness." And then God made that vision a reality.

I'm surrounded by people who evidence the fact that, as a farmer, God had a vision for what He wanted to grow on the fields of their lives.

Clearly the vision God had for my pal Steven was to take him from being a Regular Guy and turn him into a Fearless Warrior. This is a guy whose sole purpose seems to be to fight for other people's freedom. He gets into their lives, discovers what's holding them back, and does everything he possibly can to remove those obstacles. This isn't always easy, so it requires a lot of bravery. God has grown that bravery—and an "I don't care what you think about me, I just want you free" attitude—inside of Steven.

No one encourages like my wife Kristin. Seriously. When she sees someone doing something that's good, she lets them know it and tells them to keep doing it. When someone's life is headed in the wrong direction, she doesn't roll her eyes and gossip. She comes alongside them and encourages them to think differently about themselves and their lives. She's a cheerleader who's traded pompoms for wisdom and perspective. No one who knows Kristin ever feels under-encouraged. She won't let them. All because God envisioned my wife's life being that of an encourager and grew that in her.

Here's a quick list of the things God has grown in some of the people around me:

God grew a passion for helping others understand God better in my mom.

God grew steadiness and reliability in my father.

God grew faith in my mother-in-law.

God grew wisdom and compassion in my sister.

God grew trustworthiness in my brother-in-law.

God grew nurturing hearts in Sandra and Matt.

God grew an understanding of what it means to be a child of God in Jeeva.

God grew grace in Alex.

God grew a heart that can receive love in Tom.

God grew freedom in Jason.

God grew a desire to shepherd and care for people in Joel.

God grew a mother's heart in Kacey.

God grew a focus on His kingdom in Lauren.

And God's grown things in my life I'm only recently starting to identify.

He's grown confidence in me. And empathy. And maturity. Self-discipline and a better work ethic. A passion for deeper relationships.

He's also grown a perseverance in me that still amazes me because of how far I've come. (I'll be coming back to this throughout the book.)

I wasn't born with any of those things—just like most of my friends and family in the previous list weren't born with those things.

God had a vision for me. He had a vision for all of us. Then, like a good, gracious farmer, he set about growing those things inside of us.

THE CROP LIST

If God is a farmer and you are a field, what does God want to grow in you? That's not always easy to decipher. Maybe a better, easier question would be: what do *you* want God to grow in you?

Let's play pretend for a moment. What if while the farmer was out walking, the field, imagining what could be grown, spoke up. What if the field said something like, "I'd love it if you grew carrots on me!" or "How's about a peach tree?" or "Cauliflower! Cauliflower! Cauliflower!"?

And what if the farmer said, "I hear ya, field. I hear ya." And what if what the field wanted grown on it affected the vision the farmer had?

I think God allows us that. I think God actually encourages us to consider our lives, think about what good things we'd want grown (or *need* grown) in us, and ask Him for it.

Let's look at that part of the Bible where Jesus called me an evil dad in context:

> Ask and it will be given to you; seek and you will find; knock and the door will be opened to you. For everyone who asks receives; the one who seeks finds; and to the one who knocks, the door will be opened. Which of you, if your son asks for bread, will give him a stone? Or if he asks for a fish will give him a snake? If you, then, though you are evil, know how to give good gifts to your children, how much more will your Father in heaven give good gifts to those who ask him!
>
> —Matthew 7:7–11

In short, Jesus says, "Is there something good you're wanting? Ask Me for it. Period."

So my question for you is: *What do you want?*

Seriously, *what do you want?*

I'll ask again because this is a really, really important question I don't want you to gloss over—

What do you want?

What good things would you want God, the Farmer, to grow in your life . . . on your field?

What crops would make your life better? Or the lives of the people around you better?

I know. That can feel like a big, open-ended question.

Because of that, I came up with a list of things I believe God likes to grow in people. You could call them traits or abilities or gifts. But, for our purposes, I'm calling them crops.

At first glance, it will seem like a long list, but it's really not. I mean, the list of things God can grow in people is probably infinite.

This list is not infinite. If it were, this book would be *much* longer.

The list is broken up into three categories with some overlap.

Fruit of the Spirit: You're probably thinking, "Fruit?! Hey! This book is about farming so fruit makes total sense!" Thanks! I thought that was a good connection point too. In a letter Paul wrote to the Galatians (cleverly titled, "Galatians"), he said when you let the Spirit of God work in your life, fruit starts to show up. Then, he lists out that fruit.

Spiritual Gifts: These are found in Romans, Ephesians, and 1 Corinthians (Hey! Corinthians! That's us!). Paul says these gifts were placed in us before we were born—yet we can ask for them as well. These gifts are meant to help us help other people as they live their lives. A quick note: some of these Spiritual Gifts may sound confusing by name. I don't have enough space to go into each one in depth, so I'd encourage you to seek out some wise Jesus followers you trust to help you get a better understanding of some of the unclear ones.

Other stuff: This is, well, other stuff. It's a random assortment of things I've seen God grow in people. Stuff that's made their lives better. Stuff that's made the lives of the people around them better.

As you read the list, be aware of any that jump out at you. Pause if one makes you think more than any others. If one causes you to go, "Wow. I wish I had that in me," stop and write it down. And don't let any sort of weird guilt or "But what do I know?" stop you from wanting these things and asking for them.

With no further ado . . .

The Crop List

Fruit of the Spirit	Spiritual Gifts	Other Stuff
Love	Encouragement	Willingness to Obey
Joy	Giving	Endurance
Peace	Leadership	Commitment
Patience	Mercy	Generosity
Kindness	Prophecy	Maturity
Goodness	Service	Ability to Communicate
Faithfulness	Teaching	Clearly
Gentleness	Administration	Ability to Listen Well
Self-Control	Apostleship	Submission
	Discernment	Authority
	Faith	Hopefulness
	Healing	Humility
	Helping	Courage/Bravery
	Knowledge	Self-Confidence
	Miracles	Forgiveness for
	Tongues	Someone Else
	Interpreting Tongues	Forgiveness for Yourself
	Wisdom	Security in God's Love
	Evangelism	Compassion
	Pastoring/Shepherding	Optimism
	Hospitality	Focus
		Self-Discipline
		Long-Term View
		Kingdom Focus
		Masculinity/Femininity
		Sensitivity to the Holy
		Spirit
		Ability to Rest
		Happiness for Others
		Love for Yourself
		Contentment
		Gratefulness
		Empathy
		Love for God
		Selflessness
		Perseverance
		Belief
		Faith
		God's Perspective
		Strength
		Honesty
		Accurate Picture of God
		Trust
		Creativity

How different would your life look and feel if you had a single one of these crops? Or more of one of the crops that already exists in you?

What would it mean for you and how you face your life?

What would it mean for the people around you—people you're close with as well as people you will happen to meet throughout your life?

How would crops on that list help you live out your roles better? (No, not like Cordelia in *King Lear* or that time you were "Guy #3" in your pal's indie film he shot on a GoPro. By roles I mean functions you serve in various areas of your life—like being a parent or spouse or employee or student or elder or friend.)

In short, those crops are meant to bring good to you and the people around you while bringing glory to God and advancing His kingdom.

THE FARMER HUGS THE FIELD

So a farmer looks out at a field and the farmer has a vision of what could be grown on the field. He sees the promise and the end results that are possible.

The end results are all a farmer really focuses on.

An ordinary farmer looks at a field and imagines the crops he could grow. And that becomes the primary reason the farmer interacts with the field. You might say it's the only reason, really.

God's not like that with us. It's important to note this distinction, even though it exposes a breaking down of the metaphor.

When the Great Big God of the Universe looks at a Jesus follower like you and says, "I want to grow great things inside you. Things that will help you live your life. Things that will be good for you and the people around you. Things that will make you more like My perfect Son. Things that, in combination, will make you more and more a unique expression of Jesus," He's not saying, "And all of that is the reason I have a relationship with you."

What God wants to grow in you—or what you want Him to grow in you—is not the primary purpose for your interaction with God. It's not. It can't be. If it was, it'd destroy you.

I have so many great things I want to teach Mae Mae and Bomber. We'll go out and play at a park, and I'll make sure they're learning to be brave when they're facing a kiddie climbing wall or a six-foot slide. We'll read a book at night, and I'll work to get them to recognize words. We'll play with other kids, and I'll talk with them about being selfless and learning to share.

But my primary purpose in having a relationship with them and spending time with them is not so they'll be brave or learn to read or know how to be kind.

Those are secondary.

What's primary is me having a relationship with those little girls. The main reason I spend time with them is . . . to spend time with them. I want to show love to them in the midst of it all. Yes, I want them to grow in the traits that will make them "good people," but more than that I want to be close to them and to love them.

Remember: I'm an evil dad. And if an evil dad wants relationship and love more than anything else for his kids, how much more our perfect, loving Father in heaven?

Though a farmer's primary goal for a field is growth, that's not God's primary goal for you or me.

God doesn't look at us and say, "The best, highest, most important thing is for you to grow fruit of the Spirit, or new spiritual gifts, or be a good friend or neighbor or husband or wife or student or parent."

The best, highest, most important thing is for you to walk with God in this process and be close to Him and let Him be close to you and to be loved every step of the way.

That doesn't mean it's easy—it's not—but it means we're meant to consistently be reminded that God is loving to us and wants to be near to us.

Because if the primary purpose of our interaction with God was to get us to produce things in our lives, then we'd end up being utilitarian machines. This would drive us insane as we'd look at our lives—and our interactions with God—as nothing more than constant striving for better and better traits. If we didn't grow the traits the way we'd imagined, it'd rock us to our core. And if we did, we'd have a burst of ugly pride followed by, "I have to grow the next thing."

Doesn't the world tell us the purpose of life is trying to do better, try harder, reach further, acquire more? We're told the meaning of life is accomplishment.

This is no way to live. It's a terrible purpose for life because it's built on a grotesquely binary system: our lives mean something if we succeed, and they don't mean anything if we fail. This is soul crushing.

God's not a soul crusher. He comes to bring us life.

To God, the purpose of our lives isn't accomplishment. And it's not even about Him growing things in our lives so we become better people.

The purpose of life is knowing God, walking with God, living out a love relationship with Him, being loved, receiving love, letting that love radically affect our lives, and loving Him back.

God doesn't look at us and say, "You are My project."

God looks at us and says, "You are My loved child."

Imagine our farmer, going out to look at the field, envisioning what could be grown, then, kneeling down and hugging the field and saying, "Oh, field. I love you. Even if you never grow anything, I just like spending time with you."

That's weird, right?

But that's how God is with us.

And when we see Him that way, we actually free ourselves up to let Him grow the things in us He wants to grow, and we find more of a desire to join Him in that work . . . being loved in the process and loving Him back.

Not only that, but we discover that Him growing these things in us is one of the most loving things He can do, because the things He's wanting to grow in us will help us live the lives we've always imagined we could be living.

God is a good farmer.

Three Questions

Do you really believe God wants to grow great things in your life, working to make you a unique expression of Jesus in this world?

Do you believe God does this from a heart of love?

What's one item from The Crop List you want to ask God, the Farmer, to grow in your field?

Chapter 2
The Plan

I know the plans I have for you.

—Jeremiah 29:11

The Farmer takes a long pull on a dark cup of coffee as he stares out the window of the farmhouse kitchen. It's still early, but there's enough sunlight for him to get a good look at the field. He squints through the steam from his mug to take the field in. And as he stares, he considers the field.

Once he's had half his coffee and a full head of thinking, he pulls the crop list out of his pants pocket. He digs through a junk drawer and finds a piece of paper and his trusty pencil. At the kitchen table, he draws out a rough sketch of the field on the paper. Without any flourish, he simply maps out the hills, the creek, the old stump, and where he saw large rocks. After chewing on the eraser for a long moment, he proceeds to portion out the land into individual parcels. He looks over to his crop list and labels each section of the field. Corn here. Wheat there. Roses over yonder.

Satisfied with his map, the Farmer flips over the piece of paper and writes out a new list.

Remove rocks
Pull weeds
Chop stump

Put up fence

Turn ground

Plant seed

Fertilize

He lists out chores until he seems satisfied, having covered all he needs to do.

Next, he writes out the months, repeating them for a handful of years. He labels each month with either "rain" or "sun" and the expected temperatures. Then he connects some of the chores on the left with the times of the year on the right.

Finally he marks out on his makeshift calendar each crop with "Harvest Time!" next to it.

Just writing the word harvest *seems to give the Farmer joy.*

He leans back and looks over his map and his chore list and the months—and years—to come.

It's going to be a lot of work. Task after backbreaking task. Early mornings and late nights. It will require a wide variety of skills: one set to plow and plant and another to build a split-rail fence and a dozen scarecrows. There's a lot to keep straight too, as each crop demands a different order of operations and timeline to produce a healthy crop.

To anyone else, the list would look intimidating. It may even raise the question: "Is this all going to be worth it?" That question doesn't even cross the Farmer's mind. Of course it'll be worth it. He's seen the roses and the corn and the wheat and the cotton and the potatoes in his mind. Not only that, but he's vividly imagined people eating the fruits, vegetables, and bread made from the wheat, feeling the fabric made from the cotton, enjoying the smell of fresh roses in full bloom.

He's fully aware of the work and the process and the patience required. But he's also fully aware that if the field cooperates, all the effort will feel like nothing compared to the end results.

The Farmer polishes off the last of his coffee and sets down his mug. He looks back out the window at the field. He takes a deep breath. It's time to put his boots on. It's time to head out to the field. He's ready to do the work because he has a plan—a plan to bring about the promise of the field.

THE JAM AND THE DANE

Just like a farmer has a vision for a field—and all the good things he can grow on it—God has a vision for your life and all the good things He can grow in you. Hopefully, after the whole first chapter, that makes sense and you agree with the idea.

But how does all of that play out?

What good is it to have a vision if there's no plan?

Well, honestly, it's no good to have a vision if there's no plan.

Surely you know people who have big, expansive ideas for what they want to do—but absolutely no plan whatsoever to make that happen.

"I've got a great idea for an awesome app that helps people track their hair loss."

"Great idea. Sort of. How are you going to make it?"

"Eh, I don't know. I think it'll sort of just show up in the app store."

"Yeah, that's not going to happen."

"I know."

My wife Kristin and I went to a family's house for dinner a while back. When we arrived, we were told we'd be eating something called Jamaican stew. If you're like me, stew does not sound appealing. Immediately, I imagined a bubbly cauldron hanging over an open fire in a hermit's hut, full of nasty stuff like carrots, beets, and salamanders. I started looking around for bread to fill up on.

But once the Jamaican stew was served, I repented of ever questioning the goodness of Jamaican stew. This concoction was fantastic. It had about a billion different flavors that, working in concert, functioned as a hug for my mouth. I loved Jamaican stew. Kristin did too.

A few weeks later, we were hosting people for dinner and didn't know what to serve. Kristin suggested Jamaican stew. Immediately, my taste buds high-fived that idea. "Yes. We must make Jamaican stew," my tongue told my mouth to say.

We had three options when it came to making Jamaican stew.

1. Sit around on the couch hoping Jamaican stew would just appear in our kitchen in time for our guests' arrival.
2. Start putting whatever came to mind into a big pot—including carrots, beets, and salamanders.
3. Follow the recipe for Jamaican stew our friends gave us.

You may be surprised to hear this, but we went with option number three.

Why? Because we're smart enough to realize that if you have a vision for something, you can't just wish it into existence. Also, you can't just go at it willy-nilly, hoping against hope something good emerges. We know if you want a vision to become reality, you follow a plan.

I'm sure you're sitting there thinking the immortal words of Aristotle: "Duh, dude." But the fact is, many of us live our lives having a vision for the people we want to become—and that vision may even be the same God has for our lives—but we live as though we're unaware that in order for that vision to become reality, a plan has to be in place.

If you want The Jam (what I've come to call Jamaican stew), you have to follow the plan. (For the benefit of your mouth, here's the actual "plan" for Jamaican stew . . .)

Jamaican Stew (aka, The Jam)

1 lb. chicken breast
1 red pepper
1 medium-sized onion
3 garlic cloves
14 oz. can black beans (drained)
14 oz. can Rotel diced tomatoes and green chiles
1/2 c. sun-dried tomatoes
1 T. capers
1/8 c. olive oil
1/2–3/4 c. red wine (or a dark fruit juice like pomegranate, cranberry, or grape)

Jasmine or basmati rice or naan
Juice of one lime
1 bunch cilantro
Sriracha

Spices:
1 t. curry
1 t. cumin
1 t. salt
1 t. thyme
1 t. oregano
1/2 t. cayenne
Cracked pepper to taste

Combine the spices in a bowl. Dice the chicken into cubes. Mix the spices and chicken together with your hands until the chicken is evenly covered. Dice the onion and garlic. Combine garlic, onion, and oil in a large pot. Cook over medium heat until the onion is soft and fragrant. Add chicken to the pot. Add red wine/juice and simmer for thirty minutes. Add the remaining ingredients (except the rice, lime, cilantro, and Sriracha) and stir. Cook for thirty minutes to three hours on low, stirring frequently (the longer and slower the better). Serve with chopped cilantro on top, poured over rice or naan. Squeeze some lime juice on top along with a squirt of Sriracha to give it a sweet kick! Eat some. Eat some more.

You know what all of this talk about plans makes me think of? Shakespeare. That's right: Shakespeare.

In his hit play, *Hamlet* (subtitled: *How a Sad Sack Danish Guy Figured Out Who Killed His Dad and Then Moped and Then Did Something About It*), Shakespeare includes a line that's stuck with me since I first read it a long, long time ago.

Hamlet's complaining to his buddy Horatio about how hard life is.

> Our indiscretion sometimes serves us well,
> When our deep plots do pall: and should teach us,
> There's a divinity that shapes our ends,
> Rough-hew them how we will—

Of course, that makes perfect sense out of context, so let's just assume we all get what he's saying.

No! This makes no sense out of context. So, here's the Jeff Davenport Loose-and-Literature-Teacher-Offensive Translation:

> Sometimes we try to do things and we mess those things up.
> When that happens, we really should learn
> God's out there with His eye on us, keeping us on track,
> moving us toward His vision,
> Even if we're complete goofuses.

The famous Dane is articulating what I think we all know deep down: that God's working a plan that's leading up to some vision He has for our lives. "There's a divinity that shapes our ends" is a reassuring notion. It says, "God knows and God's acting—sometimes in spite of us."

Scripture goes a step further than Shakespeare. In the Bible we are not just told God is intentional about the work He does with us—we are also told He has a grand vision for each of our lives. "We are God's masterpiece" (Ephesians 2:10 NLT).

How does an artist create a masterpiece? They consider what something could become, then they take the necessary steps to turn something ordinary into something extraordinary.

A sculptor looks at a block of marble, imagines a figure, then sets about chiseling.

A carpenter considers some lumber, thinks of a table and chairs, then cuts, sands, and nails until they're real.

A trainer watches a young player with unpolished skills, then works with the player until he or she moves from amateur to pro.

When I start a speaker coaching engagement with a client—whether it's a big-wig executive, an organizational leader, or an average Joe—I have them present, assesses their strengths and weaknesses, identify their unique "speaker personality," and then I execute a custom-tailored plan to help them improve their delivery.

I don't just meet them and, without seeing them present or assessing them, go, "So don't say 'um' and move to this part of the stage when or if you happen to say the phrase 'penny whistle.' Got it?"

That wouldn't get us anywhere. Instead, I create a plan. Without a plan, they won't get better. The plan is going to help move them from Point A to Point B.

God's like this. He isn't slapdash or haphazard. He's a God of intention who acts on that intention.

THE FAKE ASTRONAUT

I've always loved movies, but I fell in love with the craft of screenwriting while I was an undergrad at Baylor University (Go Bears!). I took a class taught by The Great Brian Elliott who not only taught us how to write movies but also taught us the heart, purpose, and passion meant to be behind every script. A week into class, I knew I wanted to be a screenwriter.

After graduating, I eventually made my way to Los Angeles to get my masters in screenwriting at the University of Southern California (Go Trojans!). During the program, we learned tips and tricks on writing as well as theoretical models for screenplay structure and insights for writing different genres. At the end of our time there, each of us had to write a thesis script proving we'd actually learned something from our expensive time there.

I toiled over what to write about but finally landed on two disparate concepts that both fascinated me.

The first was NASA's Apollo program in the 1960s and those crazy, wildly courageous personalities who willingly signed on to have themselves strapped to controlled explosion machines designed to hurl a person at the moon. What would drive one of those guys? Why would he fight to go to the moon? Why would he want to be a national hero? What would be going on under the hood of someone like that?

The second was a Latin phrase I'd learned years before: *esse quam videri.* It means, "To be, rather than to seem (to be)." Read as a command, I think it means: "Don't work to try to come off as a certain type of person. Actually, authentically, *be* that person."

So I combined these two ideas into a screenplay about a troubled fictional Apollo astronaut named Wick Haley.

In my movie (called *Wick Haley*), it's the mid-1960s, and Wick Haley is the odds-on favorite to be the first man on the moon. Everyone in the country loves Wick. He's good-looking, brave, patriotic, and charming—with a warm Texas drawl to boot. Imagine Matthew McConaughey in a powder-blue NASA flight suit.

But how Wick appears on the outside is not who he is on the inside. He's actually a schemer who fights to control how his bosses, the media, and especially the public perceive him. He's driven by his selfish ambition for fame and success—and, to Wick, what's a higher mark of success than being the first man on the moon?

As I began writing, I really only knew two things: I wanted Wick to start off as a charming but duplicitous character, and by the end of the movie, I wanted Wick to have actually become the good, decent man he'd been trying to pass himself off as.

I had a vision for ol' Wick. I wanted to write a movie that was about moving him from Point A to Point B. No matter what else went into the movie—rocket ships and football and Texas and a love interest—the main reason for writing the movie was to show this character growing into someone he was meant to be.

A lot of people think screenwriting is about coming up with a plot and then writing that down. I guess that works for movies like *I'm Fast, You're Furious* or *Robots and Cars Are Cool, but Robots that Turn into Cars Are Even Cooler* or *Explosion! The Movie*, but the movies that impact you—that you remember—are less about the car chases and the kisses and the explosions and more about the main character and how they became the person they were meant to become.

Eventually I came up with a story for Wick designed to move him from a Point A to the Point B I'd envisioned for him. It's about him having to hide out in his small, Texas hometown after a public fall from grace that puts into question him being the first man on the moon. He meets people and is forced into situations that help him realize the unhealthy reasons behind his obsessive ambition and see the incongruity between the great guy he presents himself as and the self-centered egoist lurking beneath. By the end of the movie, Wick has to make a choice proving he's actually become a better person, even though it costs him what he thought he always wanted.

It wasn't enough for me, as a writer, to have an "end" in mind for Wick Haley. I also needed a plan that would bring about Wick's transformation—a transformation that would be great for him and great for every person who would encounter him the rest of his fake life.

I've written over a dozen screenplays (a few of which have been produced as TV movies), and I've found, time and time again, the only way to write a compelling story is to have a vision for the main character and then execute a plan to make that vision a reality.

Screenwriters and storytellers kind of function like God. They look at a person (or character), see them as they are, imagine a distinct vision of who they could be, then intentionally surround them by situations, people, and choices that help point them toward that new version of themselves.

Chefs, screenwriters, farmers, and God. They each have a vision . . . and they turn that vision into a reality with a purposeful plan.

So how does the plan God has to grow good things in our lives play out for us? It's helpful to me to break down God's growth plan into three different categories.

1. Maybe She's Born with It

Back in the 1990s, the cosmetics company Maybelline launched a new ad campaign. In the ads, beautiful women would walk around dark, wet streets, looking alluring, with their faces all made up. Usually, these women wore trench coats and held umbrellas while walking through misty rain because, for some reason, it seems that the fashion and cosmetic worlds in the 90s thought women looked cooler this way. As they passed men on the street, these guys would pause, look the women over and smile while shaking their heads. Then the jingle would verbalize what these men were thinking:

Maybe she's born with it?

Or . . . maybe it's Maybelline.

As if those guys—and the people watching the commercials at home—were confused. Were these women wearing makeup, or is it possible they were all born with a rare skin condition where their eyelids look like they're coated in dark green chalk, their cheeks stay impossibly rose-hued as though in a constant state of embarrassment, and their eyelashes are so heavy and long that when they blink, people nearby hear the sound of light clapping?

What if someone was born with a face that looked like it had been made up but hadn't? My wife has a face like this. She's one of those natural beauties whose features pop without aid of lipstick or mascara or blush. She was born with it.

Each of us are born with some of the items on The Crop List already grown up inside of us. It's as though God the Farmer planted seeds while we were each in the womb and those seeds had already come to fruition before we were born.

It's clear to Kristin and me that Mae Mae was born with a natural inclination to obey. That doesn't mean that anytime we tell her to do something, she hops right to it like a private in the Davenport Army. It just means that, more often than not, she seems to recognize her Mommy and Daddy as authority figures worth listening to, which translates into her doing what we ask her to.

Bomber was born with a different set of traits, including natural courage. If there had been the chance when she was one minute old, there in the delivery room, for her to jump out of the doctor's arms onto, say, a nearby ottoman, she would've done it. God made her bravery evident from Day One.

I was born like Mae Mae, with a tendency toward submission. My wife came out of the chute brimming with constant optimism. I have a friend who's always been confident. Another friend seemed to evidence empathy since she was a toddler.

Scenario number one for God and His plan to bring about a vision for your field to fruition is: He already executed the plan before you were born, so you've had that crop on your land since birth.

Okay, well . . . what do you do about that?

A couple of things. First, thank God He gave you that crop at such an early age. It's easy to overlook these kinds of crops because we take them for granted. We take them for granted because they've always existed in us. We're the fish that doesn't appreciate the water because we've always been wet.

Second, make sure you don't let these old crops die. Just because Mae Mae was born with a willingness to obey doesn't mean that will always be there. My hope is she continues growing in that (along with a number of other good traits I'm sure God wants to grow in her). I don't want Bomber to just be brave as a child. I want her to be brave all of her life. My hope (and I'm sure God's) is that Kristin stays optimistic and hopeful until her days are done. Just like there's a tendency to be ungrateful for something we've taken for granted, there's also a tendency to overlook continuing on in the traits we already have.

Now, if this type of execution of God's plan could be considered "Nature," maybe we'll file the other two under "Nurture." So here's the first of the two Nurture categories.

2. Clueless

Wick Haley had absolutely no idea there was a screenwriter out there who was manipulating events, situations, and people around him to move him from Point A to Point B. All he knew (as much as a fictional character could know) was he grew into a better man.

Sometimes that's how God's plan plays out with us. He puts things, events, situations, and people in our lives that end up producing some fruitful crop in us—all while we're ignorant to what's going on.

I grew up moving around. A lot. Six states, nine houses, and eight different schools in the span of fourteen years. That kind of constant deck shuffling did something to me as a kid.

From what I'm told, I started life as a pretty outgoing, extroverted, happy-to-talk-to-anybody kid.

But by the time I ended up at that eighth school my freshman year of high school, I was pretty tapped socially. Constantly being the new kid had caught up with me, and I started to shut down. My peers suddenly seemed intimidating, so I questioned everything I wanted to say and how well I was going to say it. This constant, overactive self-awareness made me more and more awkward. (Imagine how poorly someone would walk if they were constantly obsessing over how they were walking and how they looked while they were walking.) Because of this awkwardness, I sought out ways to avoid interactions with other people. Throughout most of high school, I kept my head down and my mouth shut so much that had there been such an award, I would've been voted, "Least Likely to Be Remembered."

Strangely enough, after graduation, I enrolled in The University of Texas at Austin (Go Longhorns!), which, at the time, had a student population of around fifty thousand. That was a lot of people . . . to avoid. Really, what in the world made an introvert like me—who wanted nothing more than to keep to himself and avoid embarrassing himself—attend one of the largest universities in the world? I honestly have no idea.

The first few months of school were incredibly painful for me. I saw people enjoying themselves at school, relaxing, and living twenty-four-hour-a-day social lives. Not me. I went to class but, immediately after, ducked back to my dorm to either be by myself or hang out with a few guys I knew from high school.

One day two of those guys told me they'd each signed up to become sports broadcasters for KTSB—the campus radio station.

A week later, I signed up to do the same thing.

Now, that's nuts. Or, actually, doubly nuts. The first level of nuts is a guy like me going to a massive, human-filled school like UT in the first place. That second layer of nuts is a guy like me signing up to sit in front of a microphone and actually speak to any of those students who could've possibly been listening.

Why did I sign up?

If you would've asked me that day, I would've either said, "I don't know," or looked down at the ground awkwardly and tried to figure out a way to get out of talking to you because, heck, I don't know who you are.

Every Sunday evening for two years, I was a part of a panel show called *Tom and Jerry's Sports Extravaganza*. Four other guys and myself would read sports scores, interview athletes, and rhapsodize about the current state of sports in America. It was . . . thrilling. Some of it was the fact I actually knew very little about sports (so there was that high-wire act of talking about something I was learning about as I went), and some of it was knowing that I, The Great Introvert of Klein High School (Go Bearkats!) was, suddenly, a broadcaster, pushing through his awkward and talking to an actual audience. (Full disclosure: *Tom and Jerry's Sports Extravaganza* had, on average, a listenership of around fifty to one hundred people.)

KTSB helped me become a little less awkward, a little less shy, and gave me a little boost of confidence.

After my second year at UT, I transferred to Baylor University and switched majors from business administration to radio/television/film. One summer in Waco, I took an actual, paying job as a DJ at KBRQ ("The Bear 102.5—Waco's Home for Classic Rock") firing off Led Zeppelin, The Police, and the Eagles into listener's cars and homes.

KBRQ continued me down a road away from shyness and awkwardness and toward confidence.

After graduating with my masters from USC, while I was writing scripts in my spare hours, I took a job as an SAT prep instructor at The Princeton Review. I'd stand in front of a group of fifty to twenty angry high schoolers who had no desire to spend their Saturday mornings or after-school hours learning how to beat a standardized test. But, over time, I actually got pretty good at it. After a few months, I found my stride and took to the front of the class with authority and figured out ways to make the classes fun, entertaining, and effective.

The Princeton Review gave me a little more confidence.

A year later I took a job as a college minister with University Ministries (UM). In no time, three hundred to six hundred college students were gathering in a church every Tuesday night to worship and hear what I might have to say about them, God, and the world. A lot of cool stuff happened for a lot of students during that time . . . but something good happened inside of me during that time too.

UM gave me even more confidence.

From UT to UM was about ten years of my life. Ten years.

I can honestly say that during those ten years, I had no idea what I was doing. I just kind of bopped around from decision to decision, doing what seemed like a marginally okay idea of what to do next.

But looking back now, I can see God was doing something in the midst of all of those half-considered decisions and difficult situations.

He saw the guy I was—shy and awkward and constantly questioning the value of his thoughts and how they would come out—and He had a vision for a Jeff who had confidence and a belief that what he had to say might be worth saying and could be said in a way that made sense and actually engaged people. Not only that, but He saw that I could actually become someone who coached other people in how to communicate more clearly and confidently.

God had a vision for growth and then executed a plan to grow good things in me—but I had no idea what was happening. I was unaware. I was clueless.

And sometimes that's okay. Sometimes that's just how God operates. He orchestrates situations and people and opportunities in our lives to accomplish particular ends, even though we don't know it's happening.

I bet that's happened in your life at some point. I bet there's a good crop that's grown up inside you, and it happened because of God executing His plan without you knowing it at the time.

Just writing all this makes me grateful God grew confidence in this way in my life.

I hope realizing what He's done in your life—even when you were unaware—makes you grateful to Him too.

Now, onto the third way God's plans could play out for us . . .

3. From Slaves to Pals

Toward the end of His time on earth, Jesus turned to His running buddies, the disciples, and said:

> I no longer call you servants, because a servant does not know his master's business. Instead, I have called you friends, for everything that I learned from my Father I have made known to you.
>
> —John 15:15

Jesus lays out two specific things. The first is that, though He used to consider humans like those fellas as slaves—people who just did what they were told by God—He'd come to think of them as friends. The second is Jesus defining the difference between slaves of God and friends of God: slaves don't know what God's doing while friends, on the other hand, do.

It'd be harsh to say it this way, but maybe I was kind of a slave during that whole radio station/Princeton Review/college ministry phase of my life. I really don't think God thought of me as Jeff the Slave, but according to this definition, I really functioned more like a slave than a friend because I was ignorant of what God was up to. (I'm not criticizing that, or ruing that I was ignorant of what was going on then. I'm just thinking about that season through the lens of what Jesus said here.)

I love that Jesus calls His buddies "friends." That's a big shift. I don't think it's so much a shift inside of God as it's meant to indicate a shift in how those dudes were meant to think of themselves. It's almost as though Jesus is saying, "Hey, guys. I bet, in the past, you thought of yourselves as slaves to God. That time is over. It's time for you to start thinking of yourselves the same way I do: as Friends of God."

Friends of God. That's such a beautiful—and wildly aspirational—idea, huh? Little, tiny, sunburn-prone, sometimes whiny, lovers of unhealthy food rather than lovers of healthy food, humans like us can be friends with Beyond Our Comprehension, Existing in All Planes, Unseen, Force of All Forces, God of Everything (Yes, Everything). That's crazy talk.

But it's just what Jesus said. And I want to think more and more of myself as a friend of God.

For me to do that, though, I have to realize that friendship with God seems predicated on Him letting me in on some of His plans.

That includes His plans for my life.

Three ways God's plans can play out in our lives: naturally so that we're born with them; through nurture, as He does things in our lives while we're blissfully unaware; and through nurture, as we're actually, somewhat, aware of what's going on.

———————

Imagine ol' Wick, down there in Haley, Texas, waiting for his shoulder and public image to heal up so he can go back to

NASA and be the first to plant the Stars and Stripes on a gray rock 240,000 miles away. What if, while writing the script, I had a way of communicating with Wick? What if he could clue into what the screenwriter of his life was doing?

Jeff: *Hey, Wick.*

Wick: *Um, where did that disembodied voice come from?*

Jeff: *I'm Jeff, Wick. I'm the guy who's writing your story.*

Wick: *I don't know what that means.*

Jeff: *Don't worry about it. Look, you're about to go through a lot of different stuff. Some things will be fun, some will be hard. But, through it all, I'm trying to do something inside of you.*

Wick: *You're what?*

Jeff: *I'm trying to grow something good in you. I'm trying to change you, getting rid of something that's not great in you and replacing it with something good.*

Wick: *I'm a pretty good guy, man.*

Jeff: *I know you think that—and you're not totally wrong— but you've also got some problems.*

Wick: *How do you know?*

Jeff: *Because I made you up.*

Wick: *Can I be done talking to you now?*

Jeff: *Wick, I'm your friend.*

Wick: *Right.*

Jeff: *And because I'm your friend, I want tell you what's going on.*

Wick: *Okay. What's going on?*

Jeff: *You care more about your reputation and appearing like a good, solid man than actually being one. You're a bit of a pretender, Wick. But I don't want you to stay that way. I like you too much. So your boss at NASA isn't going to call you back when you want him to—*

Wick: *That jerk . . .*

Jeff: *And I'm going to give you the opportunity to coach the local football team—*

Wick: *That sounds kind of fun.*

Jeff: *And you're going to meet a lady. An attractive—*

Wick: *All right!*

Jeff: *—single mom—*

Wick: *Oh.*

Jeff: *—who's going to point out some uncomfortable truths about yourself.*

Wick: *Oh.*

Jeff: *And you'll meet a kid in trouble who will need you as a father figure—*

Wick: *I'm not much of a father figure—*

Jeff: *Exactly! But all of this is going to start making you think of yourself this way. That's the point of what you'll be going through.*

Wick: *Why are you telling me all of this?*

Jeff: *Because, like I said: you're my friend.*

Wick: *I'm friends . . . with a disembodied voice?*

Jeff: *Kind of.*

Wick: *Okaaaaaay. Are we done now?*

Jeff: *Sure, Wick. But as everything's happening around you and you're meeting all of these people and you're in these different situations, would you just remember that I'm your friend and the point of all of this is to grow authentic goodness inside of you?*

Wick: *All right.*

Jeff: *Okay.*

Wick: *What do I do now?*

Jeff: *Whatever you want, I guess.*

Wick: *I thought you're the writer. You have to have me do the next thing I'm going to do.*

Jeff: *Oh yeah! Sorry . . .*

I think God rarely lays out to us every step of His plan that's going to grow things within us. But I do think there are times that, as we're in the midst of living our story, He clues us into the larger plan and the crop He's growing up inside of us.

I should say here there may be terrible, awful, painful things that have happened in your life. The Bible indicates that, one day, all of those terrible, awful, painful things will be redeemed, being used to bring about something good. Sometimes we get a sense of that redemption down here on earth. Other times, we don't. If there are terrible, awful, painful things in your past, I encourage you to ask God how they fit into this "God uses everything to bring about something good in our lives" paradigm. And, if He keeps all of that mysterious, holding back some of His plans for those things, don't try to force them into this paradigm. Instead, focus on other moments in your life that seem as more obvious means of God bringing about good for you.

A few years ago, I had an idea for a romantic comedy script I wanted to write. It wasn't the most original or amazing idea ever, but *Tour Dates* was going to be about a publicist falling in love with her client—a country music star with no interest in becoming famous. Not exactly *The Godfather*, but I thought the idea had enough merit and themes that interested me that it was worth pursuing.

I had a non-screenwriting, full-time job at the time, so I had to spend my "off hours" thinking about *Tour Dates* and jotting down ideas for scenes, characters, and situations. Once I had enough of a rough outline, I started the actual writing process.

Here's the thing you may or may not know about writing: it's hard. It's really, really hard. Someone once said writers don't like to actually write; they like to have written. That's dead-on. It's hard to come up with creative ideas. It's hard to have those creative ideas make sense. It's hard to sit at a desk with your fingers eagerly poised over the A, S, D, F, J, K, L, :/; keys, awaiting inspiration. Most of the time, I'd rather be doing something easier—like trying to stretch my ears enough so they can touch—than forcing my brain and body to write.

I wrote the first quarter of *Tour Dates*, which is, roughly, thirty pages. Thirty pages is a lot of writing. That's what I kept thinking. "That's a lot of writing, Jeff. Look at all that writing. And the words! Look at all of those words! Those are words you wrote! Great job. You've really worked hard this last month. Now, let's take a break. Like . . . a year or two."

Honestly that's how screenwriting has usually gone for me. I get an idea, I have a nice, steady stream of things I want to include in the script, I write out an outline, then I churn out the first act (which is about the first thirty pages).

Then I stop.

Sometimes for good.

Any screenwriter will tell you that writing the first act is a piece of cake compared to writing the second act. The second act (which runs from page thirty-one to ninety or so) is twice as long as Act One and about ten times as difficult. Screenwriters call it the Act-Two Slog. It's where you find your plot—the wonderful, exciting, great, promise-filled plot you established in Act One—meandering like a kid full of Benadryl wandering around a department store. It's hard to keep the Act One momentum going, it's hard to keep the character's voices consistent, and it's hard to bring the plot to the point it needs to be at as you enter Act Three. I tried writing parts of *Tour Dates*' Act Two, but those pages ended up with all the romance and humor of an oil change.

This is why my computer has, for years, been full of scripts that only go to page thirty.

But then, just as I was starting to mentally check out of *Tour Dates*, wondering what other great script I could start and not finish, I sensed God telling me something. Pushing me toward something. Urging me.

I felt as though God were saying He wanted me to finish writing *Tour Dates*.

What?

Yeah.

I knew, though, that God didn't want me to write *Tour Dates* because it was going to become some important work of art that would forever change Western Civilization. I didn't think the Smithsonian was going to request the Apple wireless keyboard "from which that great work of literature—the *Tour Dates* script—sprang forth." God wasn't saying, "Jeffrey! Thine peppy little rom-com shalt be unto the world, its well-worded savior! It surely shall save all from a fate of wrack and ruin!"

God wanted me to finish *Tour Dates* because of a prayer I'd prayed some time before.

For most of my life, whenever jobs or tasks got hard, I would quit.

In my mind, something equated "difficult" with "you shouldn't be doing this. Figure out a way not to do it."

It applied to a couple part-time jobs I had in high school. It applied to some very challenging business classes I took at UT. It applied to friendships. And it definitely applied to my writing.

A few months before the idea for *Tour Dates* popped into my head, I had come to the realization that I lacked perseverance—steadfastness in doing something despite difficulty or delayed gratification.

I started looking around my life and found the people who lived lives like the one I wanted to live—the ones who stuck with things and leveraged their skills and talents and had a lasting impact on the people around them—all had perseverance. (Not only that, but I was newly married, and I realized early that, though a lot of marriage is easy and great, to go the distance, you absolutely, totally, and completely need perseverance.)

I didn't want to lack perseverance anymore. I wanted it. And I wanted it badly.

So I asked God for it.

And it wasn't some zany, super-passionate, "Oh, Lord! Wouldst thou only giveth unto me, a super-duper dosage of that good perseverance!" It was lower-key than that. I was just thinking about my life—and all of the things I had become ashamed of not finishing—and I quietly asked God, "Would you give me perseverance, God? I think I need it. And I know I want it."

Then . . . nothing. I mean, God didn't boom from heaven and say, "Thine wish is granted!" like a cloud-dwelling genie. There was just silence. Which, at least for me, isn't uncommon after I pray.

So I went about my life.

Until . . .

Tour Dates. And God telling me to finish it.

And I knew why He was telling me to finish it: to build perseverance in me.

My story's writer was telling me, His character, "This is what I'm doing in your life."

The Farmer was telling the field, "I'm executing on my plan so I can grow a certain crop in you."

So what did I do next?

I made a bunch of excuses and did everything I could to get out of writing *Tour Dates.*

But God stayed after me. He kept impressing on me that if I wanted perseverance, this was a great way to gain it.

Every day I tried to avoid the work. Every day, God encouraged me toward it. And, on a lot of days, I actually wrote.

God even put people in place around me to keep me going. My wife (The Current World Heavyweight Encouragement Champion) gave me the space and time and "You can do this! This is good for you!" comments I needed. Pals who heard what God seemed to be saying clapped for me and goaded me on. Even articles and essays written by people I'd never met in my life all seemed to be pointing toward me finishing the script.

And you know what happened? I finished it. I totally wrote that thing.

Not only that, but I ended up rewriting it. (Any writer will tell you that, often, rewriting is harder than writing.)

Then I rewrote it four more times.

It was hard. It was so, so hard. So many days I wanted to quit. So many days I thought, "This is a waste of time." So many nights I went to bed questioning the process and why I was doing what I was doing. I'll say this: following God and doing what you feel like He wants you to do can be so, so, so hard.

But I've found . . . it's worth it.

I originally started working on *Tour Dates* because I thought it would get made into a movie, I'd make money off my writing, and I'd get more writing jobs from it—all of which are still possible as the script currently makes its way through the hands of various potential producers.

But I ended up getting something even more valuable than all of that—really and truly. I got the perseverance I'd desperately needed (for myself and for the people around me).

(Those Rolling Stones were right about getting what you need rather than what you want.)

As a friend, God told me what He was doing in my life: building perseverance in me. Because of that, I was clued in on what the Farmer was growing on my field. I wasn't ignorant, I was aware. And I wasn't passive. I was active.

THE READINESS IS ALL

Let's review the three scenarios God uses to grow something in you:

1. He does it before you were born.

2. He grows it in your life, but you don't really know it's happening at the time.

3. He tells you what He's up to, bringing you into the process.

The rest of this book is primarily about that third scenario, what the process is often like, and how we're meant to take part in that process.

A quick look back to the Bard and his deep-thinking Hamlet:

> We defy augury; here's a special providence in the fall of a sparrow. If it be now, 'tis not to come; if it be not to come, it will be now; if it be not now, yet it will come; the readiness is all.

Jeff's Unauthorized Shakespeare Reader translates that passage as:

> Believing things happen without any sort of reason is silly.
> When something happens, God is somewhere in the midst of that.
> Sometimes we don't have a clue what He's doing, or going to do—
> But that's not our business. Our business is to just be ready and responsive.

When God tells us He's going to be doing things to grow something in us—on our fields—we're meant to be ready.

When we realize God's in the midst of that process, we're meant to be ready.

When we've asked God to grow a crop in our lives, we're meant to be ready.

The readiness is all.

So what's the best way for a field to be ready?

Good soil.

Three Questions

Considering yourself objectively, what two traits from The Crop List do you think you were born with?

What's one trait you have in your life that you believe God grew in you—even though, at the time, you were unaware He was growing it?

Think about the one or two things from The Crop List you'd like God to grow in you. Is there anything you're going through right now God may be using to grow that trait in you?

Chapter 3
The Soil

Blessed is the one who trusts in the LORD, whose confidence is in him. They will be like a tree planted by the water that sends out its roots by the stream.

—Jeremiah 17:7–8

The Farmer sticks his hand down into the earth, wriggling his fingers to get down deeper, then pulls up a handful of dirt. He examines it closely, taking a good, long look at the dark mass. Holding it close to his face, he inhales deeply, smelling it. He brings a chunk up close to his eye, looking it over like a jeweler investigating a diamond. He rubs bits of it between his fingers, feeling for moisture, texture, and any little nits or grubs that might be in there.

He drops the dirt back to the earth and walks another fifty paces farther into the field. Does it all again.

He repeats this a number of times until he has a good record of the ground throughout the field.

He wants to know how receptive the field will be to what he wants to grow and how he'll grow it.

He knows it needs good soil.

Without good soil, he knows his work will be subject to frustration, and the likelihood of healthy crops will be minimized.

That afternoon, the Farmer travels into town and picks up a few things he knows will help make the soil healthier and ready to turn seed into yield.

He fills the back of his pickup truck with bags and bags of chicken and horse manure. It smells awful, but he knows it's brown gold when it comes to farming.

After dropping the bags off at the field, he travels back to town and buys a ton-and-a-half of mulch—decaying leaves and bark.

Then, he goes around to the back of the farmhouse and admires a smelly, fly-ridden ten-foot mound. It's a collection of old food scraps—everything any normal household would've tossed down the kitchen sink disposal. To the Farmer, this pile of compost represents a turbo engine for crop growth.

Over the next few days the Farmer scatters the smelly manure around the field.

He also covers areas that seem to have the weakest soil in the mulch.

Then he peppers the composting across the entire acreage.

Finally he digs small furrows to sluice away any excess rain that might fall.

After a long, hard, backbreaking week, he leans on his shovel and looks out at the field. He knows all he's done to the field is setting it up for success.

Because of the manure and composting, the soil's nitrogen levels will increase dramatically, making it perfect for receiving seed, feeding it, and turning it into a vibrant crop. Because of the mulch, the soil will be protected from extreme temperatures and other inclement weather. And because he dug the trenches, heavy rains won't wash away the soil's richness.

The field is ready to grow because the soil is ready.

FIFTY SQUATS

Growing good things in us isn't always an easy process. It usually requires God challenging the way we normally do things, upturning some of the ways of thinking we've come to hold dear, or encouraging us to face down situations or undertakings that seem difficult or even painful.

I'm not saying it's all a terrible, awful slog—there will be times of joy in the midst of the process—but parts of it are tough. Think of the almost violent nature of a seed breaking through the soil. That soil gets pulled apart and cracked open as the seed is planted and, later, as the seed makes its way up through the ground, toward the sky.

So how can we focus on "readiness" (as Hamlet sayeth)? How can we position our minds and hearts so we're receptive to what God's doing and ready to play our part in the process? How can we have the right soil that (as we'll see later) Jesus talks about in Matthew 13?

Despite a deep-seated loathing for exercise, I started taking some workout classes at our local gym a few years ago. The classes were only an hour each. I thought, "I can do anything for an hour." I'd show up, jog in place or whatever it is I was supposed to do, get my heart rate up, sweat enough to tell myself I was really "going for it," dab my brow with a fluffy white towel, then go home, satisfied I'd magically added a week or so to my lifespan.

This was not how it went.

This class was hard.

Wait. *Hard* is not a strong enough word. Let's look at *Roget's Big Book of Words that Mean the Same Thing as Other Words* and see if there's a better word.

Arduous? Strenuous? Laborious? Herculean?

Yes. This class required Herculean effort.

Our instructor was an intense woman/gulag guard named Becca. Becca had a fierce, extreme ponytail—if one hair got lose from that pony tail, I got the sense it would loudly go, *"BOING!"* like a busted spring in a cartoon. Becca had a fierce, extreme glare—ideal for staring down anyone who wasn't keeping up with her insane tempo. Becca had a fierce, extreme shape—it was clear that all she did, all day long, was eat carrots and do lunges. Becca wore fierce, extreme make-up—she seemed to dare it to run while she was exercising (*"I dare you, Maybelline"*).

Becca's class destroyed me. That I-can-do-anything-for-an-hour attitude lasted for about 21.3 seconds. My expected "light beads of sweat" quickly turned into an "embarrassingly torrential outpouring from every possible sweat gland on my body making my shirt look like I'd put it on straight out of the washing machine" state.

The worst were the squats. Oh man. *Squats.*

Up-down-up-down-up-down.

Every bit of my weight being forced up and down my poor, ill-suited thigh muscles.

Becca seemed to like doing squats in the same way I like eating Milk Duds. ("One more? Sure! Why not! These are great!")

And she had us do fifty.

Fifty squats.

In case you're wondering how many squats that is: it's fifty times as many squats as one squat.

I didn't last long in Becca's class. I only went a handful of times.

Why? Mostly because I didn't like doing hard exercises.

But the deeper reason may have been this: I didn't know Becca. I wasn't buddies with Becca. Aside from her having all the grace and kindness of the warden in *The Shawshank Redemption*, I didn't know much about her. Why should I have believed her when she told me squats were good for me? What qualifications did she have? And, to top it all off, she didn't know me. The most she knew about me was that I was some dude, panting in the back of the room, looking like he'd walked through a car wash on the way over.

I bailed on Becca's class because I lacked one thing: trust. I didn't trust Becca.

In the same way, trust is the one thing we need more than anything else when it comes to being ready for God to do the things in us that are going to bring about good crops.

Trust is a word that appears all throughout the Bible. It's identified as the key to going along with Jesus' plans for His people and for the world. We're told to trust God. Trust in Jesus. Trust what God is up to. Trust and obey. Trust fall into Jesus' big, burly arms.

Sadly, the idea of "Trust God" has become a bit of a dead cliché. It hardly means anything anymore. Or it sounds offensive and trite because it's used by well-meaning people to tell you everything will be okay, even in the midst of awful circumstances. When that happens, you roll your eyes like they're dice on a craps table.

Though I hate how it's become a cliché, I do think the notion of trust is vital and paramount to us growing in any area at all with God. So let's dig a little deeper into the concept of trust.

Trust is believing in something so firmly you act in a way that proves you believe it.

For our purposes, trust means that as God works to grow good things in you, you believe He's doing the right thing and so, when the process is challenging, you go, "Well, this is no fun, but it's gonna end up good," and when He asks you to do something to further the process, you go, "I may not necessarily want to do that, but I'll try to do it because I trust God and what He's doing."

If a client doesn't trust me as a speaker coach, we'll be wasting our time. I'm going to ask them to do a lot of things that will feel odd or uncomfortable to them. I'm going to push them to deliver in front of an audience in a way that's not their natural way of delivering. In the end, that pushing will make them a better speaker. But if they don't trust me, they won't let me push them. They'll keep delivering how they've always delivered. Ultimately, they won't improve.

Let's dig a little deeper and try to figure out what's beneath the surface of truly trusting God. What powers the trust machine?

Trust is built on two things. And when we believe those two things, trust happens.

THE GUY IN THE PICKUP TRUCK

Imagine you're walking along a sidewalk minding your own business. A vehicle pulls up to the curb. You look over. It's a white Toyota Tacoma pickup truck with a Texas license plate. You glance over as the window goes down. Inside, you see the guy who's driving. He's a sturdy-looking man of sixty with gray hair, glasses, and brawny hands. After a moment he says, "Get in."

What do you do?

I can tell you what I'd do: I'd hop in. No questions asked. Wouldn't you?

No, you probably wouldn't.

Why would I get in, but you wouldn't?

Or, put another way, why would I trust that guy but not you?

Probably because that guy's not your dad.

But he's my dad.

I've known David Darryl Davenport all my life.

Growing up, Dad encouraged me, provided for our whole family, led our family, and made sure I knew how proud he was of me.

Once I left the house, Dad continued to encourage me and help me and serve as a wise guide for me.

David Darryl Davenport has shown love to me every day of my life.

Why would I trust the guy in the pickup truck? Because I know he loves me. He's proven his love to me by all the things he's said to me and all that he's done for me. I don't question Dad's love for me. So when he says, "Get in," I get in.

If I didn't think he loved me, I wouldn't come near that truck.

Or if I thought he loved me, but I wasn't totally sure . . . if my dad wasn't a really great dad but more of a fickle guy who sometimes cared for me and sometimes didn't and did things more out of selfish motives than for my own ultimate good . . . then, at the least, I'd be hesitant about getting in the truck. I might get in, but I'd be nervous the whole time, keeping my hand on the door handle in case he takes a turn I don't like so I can jump out of the moving truck.

If I don't believe my dad loves me, I won't trust him.

If I believe my dad loves me, I'll trust him.

In the same way . . . if I don't believe God loves me, I won't trust Him.

If I believe God loves me, I'll trust Him.

We can truly want to trust God and His process for growing good things in our lives, but if there are cracks in what we believe about His love for us, our trust will fall apart. Even if we rationally think, "He's a Great Big God Who Made Everything, so even though I don't believe He loves me, personally, I'm still gonna trust Him," that trust won't last very long.

And the scale of the love of God we believe in has to be huge. Like, really, really big. Or, put more accurately, unlimited. Check out this great Bible verse. It's from Paul and written to a group of people about God's love and how they should be rooted in it (*Rooted!* Like a plant! In a field!)—

> I pray that you, being rooted and established in [God's] love, may have power, together with all the Lord's holy people, to grasp how wide and long and high and deep is the love of Christ, and to know this love that surpasses knowledge— that you may be filled to the measure of all the fullness of God.
>
> —Ephesians 3:17–19

Paul's instructing the people to know every bit of this love— but here's the thing: God's love is too big to know every bit of it! And he's instructing you, little human being person, to be filled up with as much of it as would fit Great Big Giant Creator God. You can't do it, can you? No! His love is too big!

If your belief in the love of God is limited in size, then it's going to either immediately or over time cause cracks in your trust.

Do you believe God's love is contingent upon your behavior, performance, or (this is ironic) your level of trust in Him? If so, then your understanding of His love is limited and, really, reliant on you and your efforts—not on Him, what He's done for you, and His kindness. That's not what God tells us about

His love through the Bible—God says His love is unlimited, not based on what we accomplish or fail to accomplish, on what we've done or left undone.

It's important to know this love isn't always a comfortable, peaceful-easy-feeling love, though. God's love—like any real and true and deep love—sometimes pushes you and leads you into places that can feel painful. But these places will eventually be good for you.

When I turned sixteen, my dad told me I needed to get a job. Now, as a sixteen-year-old, the idea of getting a job sounded like a bad idea on the same level as New Coke or *George* magazine. Clearly my dad was making money—we had food on the table and cars in the drive—so why did I need to? Seemed like me getting a job would be repetitive. Why would both of us need a job?! Also, think of Dad! I don't want to step on his toes. He's the breadwinner! I don't want to compete with Dad!

But of course that was all dumb. Dad didn't want me to get a job so I could bring $3.25 an hour to our family's bank account. He wanted me to get a job to learn responsibility and commitment. So I got a job at Loew's Theater as a movie usher. (The concept of "movie usher" may have once seemed glamorous—a guy in a vest and tie, showing the local swells to their seats with a flashlight. But by the time I got my job at a movie theater, "usher" really meant, "Guy who cleaned up concession trash after the eighth showing of *Teenage Mutant Ninja Turtles 12*, refilled the toilet paper in the bathrooms, and picked off black Jujyfruits ne'er-do-wells had stuck to the seat backs.")

I didn't want to get that job—or keep it—but I knew it was good to do because I knew Dad loved me and wasn't just being arbitrary about what he was telling me to do.

I trusted him. Why? Because I knew he loved me, and what he was telling me to do came from that love.

God's the same way. His love is big and wide, but it's also challenging and wild. As C. S. Lewis writes in *The Lion, the Witch and the Wardrobe* of Aslan (the lion character meant to represent Jesus): "'Course he isn't safe. But he's good."

It's not that God is wily or careless. It's that He's loving and intentional. And sometimes that love leads us to places that could challenge us or cause some pain and discomfort.

I heard a song about two decades ago that's stuck with me ever since. It's by a crazy, wild-eyed Jesus-follower named Rich Mullins. Rich was pretty nuts (look him up) and saw God in a way nobody else writing pop songs about God seemed to. He had a song that was simply titled, "The Love of God." Now you might think a song called "The Love of God" would go something like:

> God, you really love me
> I know because of things like rainbows and butterflies
> And hamburgers with cheese
> You give me heavenly hugs by showing me the moon
> And cute, snuggly, big-eyed ponies

But that's not how Rich describes God's love in his song. Instead he describes God's love as a "reckless, raging fury." Referring to the love of God as a reckless, raging fury is slightly different from comparing it to naps in the sun and unicorn kisses.

But I think Rich learned—by trusting Him—that being loved by God was a pretty wild thing.

And I've come to learn this as well.

And I think I'll learn it more and more as I continue to receive His love.

Honestly I could go on and on for a hundred more pages about God's love. There's so much to it, and I really believe it's the crux of all of life. As my pal Steven says, "God's love is like the top button on your shirt. If you don't 'get it'—if you don't really believe He fully, totally, and completely loves you without reservation—then the buttons that come after it—everything you'd try to do with God or for God, or for other people, or whenever you try to obey or 'behave'—will be totally out of whack. You have to have that 'God's love' button right."

(For more on God's love, would you do yourself a favor and check out the writings and talks of Brennan Manning? Read *The Ragamuffin Gospel*. I know people tell you all the time about books that changed their lives, but let me say: that book really changed my life.)

Here's another great line from ol' Clive Staples Lewis about God's love: "[The Jesus-follower] does not think God will love us because we are good, but that God will make us good because He loves us."

If trust has two legs holding it up, the first one is love.

NOT THE BEST HEALTHCARE

A couple years back, I was doing something around the house, and I banged my elbow. Hard. Really hard. I let out a yell. I didn't think it was broken, but it sure felt like something was wrong in there. Thankfully, I didn't have to go far to get my elbow checked out.

I told my care provider what happened. She listened and then looked at my elbow. After a long moment, she walked away to get something.

When she returned, she was smiling wide, holding something in her hand. It was a used Band-Aid with rocket ships on it.

"This will really help you." Then she put the Band-Aid on my elbow. "You're all better. Okay." Then she walked away.

My "care provider" was my four-year-old daughter Mae Mae. At the time, she was big into playing doctor, all because she had a fake veterinarian toolkit she thought qualified her to practice medicine on actual humans.

She'd also fallen in love with Band-Aids (as four-year-olds do), not realizing Band-Aids lose both their cuteness and efficacy after they've already been used.

For Mae Mae, all problems—banged elbows, headaches, bad moods—could be cured with Band-Aids.

Nothing against Mae Mae and her burgeoning medical practice (she has a great bedside manner and seems to really care), but she's not the best doctor I've ever seen.

Please don't tell her, but I don't trust her medical opinion. (Also, she doesn't take my insurance.)

Why don't I trust her?

Is it because I don't think she loves me?

No! This little girl loves me like nobody's ever loved their daddy. I mean, the kisses and the apropos-of-nothing "I love you, Daddy!"s and the hugs and the snuggles are without end. This girl loves me. Period. Hands-down. End of discussion.

But if she loves me, then why don't I trust her?

Because of the other leg that holds up trust.

That leg is wisdom.

I really don't believe in the wisdom of Mae Mae. At least not yet. To be fair, how much wisdom can someone gain in four years? Not much, honestly.

She knows left from right and how to turn on *Daniel Tiger's Neighborhood* and how to say apple in Spanish, but that's kind of the upper limit of her understanding.

Dr. Gregory is my real doctor. He's not nearly as cute as Mae Mae, but he's been practicing medicine for more than twenty years. He's seen a thousand cases of this, that, and the other and doesn't have to open up WebMD on his computer to figure out what's wrong with me. He just knows. He's wise.

Because he's wise, I'm more prone to trust him than Mae Mae.

To truly trust God, you have to believe He's completely wise. You have to believe He's seen things you've never seen, He understands things you'll never understand, and His perspective is so, so, so much wider and better than yours.

There's a skyscraper in Minneapolis I go to pretty often. There's a conference room on the thirty-second floor that's massive and has an entire wall of ten-foot-tall windows. When I stand there and look out, I can practically see to Nebraska.

Let's say I'm up there and I see a tornado coming. Then let's say I call someone who was working on the second floor. "Hey," I'd say, "there's a tornado coming. We should all head down to the underground parking structure."

Let's say my friend on floor two is, well, arrogant. Let's say they look out their window for the tornado. Because they're on the second floor, other skyscrapers block their vision. They see bits of the clouds but not the funnel cloud headed our way.

Who has more wisdom? My friend with a limited perspective or me with my big, wide, high-up perspective?

Because I can see more, I have more wisdom and should, therefore, be trusted. My friend should probably trust me because I can see a tornado coming, even if he can't see it himself.

I think we can agree that God has a pretty good perspective. Now, I'm not referring to Him sitting up on a really tall chair, at the top of a really tall staircase, way up high above the clouds in heaven. His perspective isn't great because of that.

He has a good perspective because He's seen all of time unfold. And He knows every piece of every process that's in motion. He knows what's going on with every human. He knows how all of the parts work together. He knows who is where, what their desires are, and what drives them. He sees it all.

If we agree God's perspective is infinite, then we could conclude His wisdom is infinite.

That's a lot of wisdom.

Much more than mine.

The Bible says, "The foolishness of God is wiser than human wisdom" (1 Corinthians 1:25).

That's a poetic way of saying that the best efforts of humans to be smart pale in comparison to God's wisdom.

From a purely logical standpoint, I get that. Of course little, human me isn't as sharp as Big Giant God. But I don't always let that logic lead me toward belief. I definitely respond to Big Giant Wise God with actions and responses that seem to indicate I'm Big Giant Wiser Jeff. I don't want to do that, but I do. And when I do, I undercut that important, second part of trust: believing God is wiser than me.

A NEW INSTRUCTOR

For us to trust God, we need to believe in both His heart and His brain. We need to believe He totally, completely, and unconditionally loves us, and we need to believe He's infinitely wise, seeing every aspect of every situation and issue, understanding the things we don't even know we don't understand.

We need both legs—a belief in His love and wisdom—for trust to move us forward.

If we believe in one of the two, but not the other, trust falls apart.

But if I believe in both, I'll trust Him more, and when He leads me through difficult situations or directs me toward challenges, I won't be as likely to shrink back. With trust in God that's built on belief in His love and His wisdom, I'll go with Him where He wants to go, and the crop He wants to grow in me will come about more easily.

After I gave up on taking Becca's exercise classes, a new teacher came to the gym. This teacher was every bit as fit as Becca but was much cuter, actually smiled, and had a ponytail that didn't look like it was tight enough to pop the top of her head off.

It was my wife.

Kristin taught the same basic class as Becca, but when Kristin taught the class, I got so much more out of it. With her at the front of the class, I was more prone to stick it out the entire hour, to push myself, and to become a little more fit.

Why?

Because I knew this instructor. I knew she'd taken human physiology classes in college. I knew she had gone to nursing school. I knew she'd been trained to teach these classes. I knew she knows what exercises did what, how they affected a body, and in what ways they should be done properly.

But her wisdom isn't just limited to general kinesiology.

Kristin also knows all about me. She knows I have a bum knee that screams like a middle school kid in a haunted house every time I overwork it. She knows that if I overdo it in a class, I'll be less likely to come back for the next one. But she also knows that I'm not good at pushing myself and that I give in too easily. She knows I respond to being pushed—but being pushed in a certain way.

Also, Kristin loves me. Nobody else in the class has that connection with the teacher. Sure, she was kind to everybody in class and seemed to really care whether or not they were doing their best for those sixty minutes, but I was the one who got the "looks"—those moments when Kristin would glance at me and smile and nod as though to say, "You're doing great. I'm proud of you. Keep it up."

Kristin was happy everyone was there for her class. But she was really glad I was there—because she cared about me and my health. She knew it was good for me. She pushed me because she loved me.

Because I believe Kristin is wise and loving, I came to really love going to exercise class. And, over time, I was able to do all fifty of those stinking squats.

REMINDERS

Good soil is all about trust.

And trust is belief that God loves you and He's totally wise.

To some degree, we all probably get that . . . but it's easy to forget.

So what's a field to do?

Remind itself. That's what a field is supposed to do.

I'm a big notecard guy. If I have to wake up early for something, I write what I need to wake up for on a notecard, fold it up like a little tent, and put it on my alarm clock. That way, when 5:00 a.m. rolls around, I don't mindlessly turn off the alarm because I can't recall why in the world I'd set my alarm for such an unkind hour.

I put notecards everywhere. According to a recent USGA survey, roughly 70 percent of my desk is covered in notecards with little reminders written on them. They say things like,

"Call Ben" and "Oil Change on Friday." But then there are several that have statements on them that aren't telling me to really do anything.

"God's love isn't dependent on you."

"Give God a little credit. He may know what He's doing, even if you don't think so." (That's something my friend wrote to himself on Twitter, and I stole it for myself.)

And I also have Bible verses on notecards.

> As the heavens are higher than the earth, so are my ways higher than your ways and my thoughts than your thoughts.
>
> —Isaiah 55:9

> I pray that you, being rooted and established in love.
>
> —Ephesians 3:17

> I no longer call you servants . . . I have called you friends.
>
> —John 15:15

I'm a forgetful guy, honestly. What's sad is I'm better at remembering tasks I need to do than core truths meant to drive my life. So I write those notecards. And I see them at times when I seem to need them most.

I try to read a bit of the Bible every day for a number of reasons, but the primary one seems to be to remind myself.

I've been following God for a long, long time. I heard about God's love and wisdom the first time a long, long time ago. And yet . . .

. . . I seem to act as though I've forgotten it all the time.

So I read.

And when I find a verse or phrase that really captures something about God and myself, I write it on a notecard.

Because I don't want to logically believe in God's love and wisdom only to forget about it—

—especially during the times when I need to know it—really know it—the most.

I want to trust God. I need to trust God. And only by being in touch with His love and wisdom daily do I get the trust I need.

What's a farmer looking for when he walks out to look at his field, to see if it's ready to grow good things? He's looking at the condition of the soil. He wants to see if it's ready to receive and go through something that can be difficult but will also produce crops.

God's the same way. He looks at us—at our "soil"—to see if we're ready. That readiness is trust. And trust is predicated on believing God is completely wise and totally loving. If I don't trust Him, I'll be like a field with a gag reflex, coughing the seed back up after it's been planted. If I trust Him (at least as much as I possibly can in that moment), He's ready to go ahead with His plan—which may include steps I may not understand or situations I may question—to grow good things in me for my benefit and the benefit of everyone I encounter.

Three Questions

What's one thing that stops you from believing God is totally wise?

What's one thing that keeps you from believing in God's complete love for you?

How would your life look differently if you believed God was totally wise and loved you completely?

Chapter 4

The Obstructions

The rough ground shall become level, the rugged places a plain. And the glory of the LORD will be revealed.

—Isaiah 40:4–5

With the taste of coffee still in his mouth, the Farmer makes his way to the barn behind the house. He eyes a massive pegboard holding a variety of tools and implements. He grabs a pointed shovel and lays it in an old wheelbarrow.

And a heavy pickaxe. And a sledgehammer. And a heavy, curved-handled axe. And a tattered burlap sack. And a chain. They all go in the wheelbarrow.

As he turns to exit the barn, he spots a pair of toughened, leather work gloves. He grabs them and shoves them into the pocket of his overalls.

Not twenty yards from the barn, the Farmer stares down his first challenge: a thick and angry tangle of briars and brush. It's a mass of thorns and thistles twisted into a clump like a pile of poorly stored Christmas tree lights. The Farmer puts on the gloves and shoves his hands into the mess. He reaches deep, deep, deep down into the brambles. The farther he reaches in, though, the closer his neck and face get to the sharp thorns. They scrape and claw at every inch of his exposed skin. Still, the Farmer reaches in deeper.

Finally he gets his fingers around the base of the brush—the spot where it reaches up out of the earth. He grips tightly and pulls. It doesn't budge. He can tell this thing isn't about to let go without a fight. He repositions his legs to get better leverage. He pulls—hard. The briars still won't let loose their tether to the dirt. The Farmer doesn't give up, though. He stays at it. And, eventually, his strength bests the brush's lifeline to the earth—its root system. The dry earth breaks apart, and the weed lets go. As it does, the Farmer falls over backward . . . with a smile on his face. The thicket has been released.

He throws the brush into the burlap sack. He's succeeded, but he doesn't stop to celebrate or dust himself off. There's no point. He's only going ten steps where he'll repeat the process with another batch of scrub brush. And beyond that, another. And another. It will take time, but He's committed to getting these nasty, fruitless weeds out of the spots he's designated as ideal crop growth places.

He knows that if he plants seeds without pulling up the weeds, the weeds will take the seedlings over, choke them out, and keep good fruit from ever being produced. And if he just pulls the tops off or cuts them with a blade without getting down to the roots, the weeds will just come back stronger than before.

Eventually he gets to his next task: a large boulder, sticking up out of the earth in the middle of a flat meadow. He plops the wheelbarrow down next to it and peers closely at the rock. It's huge. A good seven feet in diameter with a least half of it stuck down into the dirt. There's a patch of green moss on the south-facing side. The massive rock must weigh five, six hundred pounds.

But the Farmer's no more intimidated by this than he was by the brush. He pulls the shovel out of the wheelbarrow.

Then, with the sun beating down against his neck, he digs the shovel into the dirt at the base of the rock. It goes in a few inches. The earth is hard here. The Farmer steps his foot onto the shovel head and leans in. The spade goes in slightly further. He leans the shovel back and removes a clump of dirt. Throws it to the side. Another two inches of the rock is exposed. But two inches isn't a lot considering the size of the entire thing. This is going to take a while.

The Farmer has to go at the dirt all around the rock. He stabs it with the shovel, pitching the shovel back and forth, pushing for all he's worth. He works lose another chunk of earth. Throws it aside. His sweat soaks the dry dirt all around him. He doesn't stop. He won't stop until the ground is free of the rock.

As he gets deeper and deeper into the ground, he finds a spot where the dirt just won't give way. A ledge of rock is stubbornly wedged. He pulls the pickax from the wheelbarrow. He swings it. Trink. Trink. Trink. *The ground fractures. It crumbles into thick, dry hunks. He turns again to his shovel. Removes the dirt. He repeats this process over and over again.*

When he's cleared enough earth to expose most of the rock, he turns to his sledgehammer. Krunk. Krunk. Krunk. *A crack appears. The Farmer continues, swinging and swinging until the rock breaks apart.*

Eventually the massive boulder is reduced to a pile of rubble. He fills the wheelbarrow with the rocks, walks it back to a worn path leading from the barn to the farmhouse, and dumps it. Goes back for more. Does it all again. Slowly, the useless, massive boulder becomes a gravel pathway.

Before he moves on to his next job, the Farmer looks into the hole where the boulder once sat. He kneels down to investigate the soil that had surrounded the rock. He sees bright colors and specks of white in the dirt. He nods and smiles, knowing those are signs of important minerals left behind by the boulder that will help feed the crops he'll end up planting in that spot. What was once blocking growth will soon help it.

Then there's the stump he spied when he'd first looked over the land. The stump is even bigger than the rock. The wood is dark and charred. Looks like what was once a mighty oak tree was felled years ago by a lightning strike. He sizes up the stump then reaches for his curved-handled axe.

Chop. Chop. Chop. *He works the stump over for a few hours then switches to a different task.*

He does the same thing the next day.

Then the next.

This goes on for some time—a little each day—because the Farmer knows it shouldn't be done in one fell swoop. He has too much admiration for the remains of the once mighty oak to just tear it up all at once.

After a week or so, though, he's unloosed the massive tree's base from the log-sized roots sticking into the ground. He wraps a chain around it and hooks the chain to the back of his truck. He starts up the truck, puts it in first gear, and pulls forward. As he does, the stump shifts. He stops and starts, stops and starts, over and over again until, finally, the earth is finally freed of the stump.

He gets out to look at the stump, now lying on its side.

Its full size surprises even him. The root system looks like a thatch of wooden octopi. He removes the chain. Nods in respect to the fallen tree. Then picks up the axe again. "I'll make good of you. I will," he says. As he chops the stump into pieces, he imagines them being fed into the wood-burning stove in the house, the fence posts he can craft from them, and the cross beams perfect for building scarecrows. In the Farmer's mind, the tree rises from the dead.

Eventually the Farmer sleeps, satisfied with all he's done. The brush has been cleared, the rock is gone, and the mighty oak stump has been repurposed. He rests well, knowing the field is better off now. Much better off.

A "LEAST-WANTED" LIST

Like the farmer, God has a vision for great things He wants to grow in our lives. Things that are good for us and the people around us. To make that vision a reality, He has to execute a plan. That plan can only truly take effect if the soil is ready. Along with ensuring the soil's readiness, the Farmer often has to remove obstructions—things that block the good from growing—the rocks, weeds, and stumps in our lives.

It can feel surprising, disconcerting, and even painful.

A field doesn't necessarily have a personal connection with rocks or weeds or stumps. But we usually have a deeply personal connection with the obstructions in our lives. That's what can make their removal so challenging.

Because of this, when God the Farmer comes along and says, "Hey . . . for your own good, I want to get rid of this thing in your life," it can be nerve-wracking to give him the go-ahead.

I can tell you from personal experience, though, that in the end, it's worth it. Letting go of those rocks, weeds, and stumps for corn, wheat, and roses is a worthwhile exchange.

So what are rocks, weeds, and stumps in our lives? Here's a nice, sterile way of thinking of them:

1. Rocks: Beliefs and habits that keep good stuff from beginning to grow.

2. Weeds: Beliefs and habits that allow good stuff to grow for a while but then choke it out, killing it.

3. Stumps: Beliefs and habits that used to be good for our land but aren't anymore.

Getting specific, though, can be a sensitive endeavor. Again, we're all usually attached to the obstructions in our lives. We've grown accustomed to them and probably don't recognize them as impediments to growth.

Following is a list of possible obstructions. I put this list together after thinking about my own life as well as the lives of friends and various people I've met with over the years. Know this, though: I probably don't know you. So I don't necessarily know what's an obstruction in your life and what's not. You may have obstructions in your life God wants to remove but may not be on this list. My hope is this list jogs your mind and God uses it to point you to an obstruction in your life He wants to address. So ask God to show you if there is an obstruction and what that obstruction may be.

Possible Obstructions to Growth

⊙ A bad dating relationship or friendship

⊙ A job that's not good for you

⊙ Addictions

⊙ Obsessions

⊙ Destructive thinking about yourself

⊙ Wrong motivations

⊙ A tendency to settle for less than God's best

⊙ Seeing yourself differently from the way God sees you

- ⊙ Any sort of idol (something that takes precedence above God and His good plans for you)
- ⊙ An old relationship you idealize—even though it's over
- ⊙ Doing good things because you're trying to earn God's approval or love
- ⊙ People-pleasing
- ⊙ Comparing yourself to others
- ⊙ Desire to control
- ⊙ Shame
- ⊙ Pride
- ⊙ Unforgiveness

Did anything on that list jump out at you? Did anything point you toward something else—not on the list—that could be an obstruction?

I can't dive into every obstruction on that list, but I do want to look more closely at what I've found to be the three most common obstructions in people's lives. These are the ones people have pointed out to me as their most common hindrances whenever I've used the field metaphor. Each of these can serve as either rocks (stopping growth from starting), weeds (killing off existing growth), or stumps (things that used to be good but are now stopping growth).

THE WRONG PERSON

People are great, right? (I'm an introvert, so that's an actual question. Ha!)

They're part of the deep fabric of life, connecting us to other humans with deep and lasting bonds, reminding us that, in fact, God doesn't want us to be alone.

But our relationships can frequently give us trouble. This happens most often when we're in a relationship with someone who I'll refer to as The Wrong Person.

The Wrong Person could be someone you're friends with yet that relationship is stymying your growth, keeping you from becoming the person God wants you to be.

Or The Wrong Person could be someone you're dating. And this relationship is, for some reason, holding you back and hindering God's growth in you.

Let's think about The Wrong Person friendships first.

In most cases, friendships actually help us become better people. A good friend isn't just someone I bowl with or watch German Expressionist films with or make quilts with. A good friend is also someone who encourages me to be my best self, pursuing the things God has for me, pointing out places where I may be struggling without recognizing it, and helping me act like the person I'm meant to be.

A good friend is someone you enjoy being around and who helps make you a better person.

Sometimes, though, we get tied into a friendship with The Wrong Person. These are the friendships that hinder our growth, cause us to act less like the person we're meant to be, and steer us in the wrong direction. The Wrong Person friendship may start off being a Right Person friendship and devolve over time, or it could start as a Wrong Person friendship right off the bat.

These friendships are common in high school. That guy who's egging you on to get drunk and climb up to the top of a five-story parking structure to see if you can fly? That guy's probably The Wrong Person. The girl who's discovered that sleeping around makes her feel secure—at least for twenty minutes at a time—and wants you to do that too? She's probably The Wrong Person.

Those Wrong People exist beyond high school; they're just not as easy to spot.

That close pal who's become more and more driven by chasing money and job status and acts like you're "behind" if you're not actively pursuing dough and a promotion could be a Wrong Person friend.

That person who's reset their priorities so that growing, and loving, and helping have taken a backseat to living out her selfish desires—and who wants you to reorder yourself in the same way—could be a Wrong Person friend.

The friend who can't engage with you about the crops God wants to grow in you and who seems frustrated that's such a high priority for you could be The Wrong Person.

These friendships go wrong when they influence you in a way that you start moving in the wrong direction.

This influence is often very, very subtle. You hardly notice it's happening. It just starts to change you, over time, slowly.

Now God doesn't just want us to be friends with people who are always making the right decisions and encouraging us to do the same. I think He wants us to be friends with people who aren't always making the right decisions too. The difference between this kind of friendship and a Wrong Person friendship is that a Wrong Person friendship actively moves us, and our lives, in the wrong direction. This is the kind of friendship that keeps God from growing new things in you or undercuts the growth He's started in you.

I've had to cut ties with friends in the past because I started to recognize that, after I hung out with them, I had a tendency to act in ways that weren't what God wanted for me. I'm not talking about spray painting overpasses or crank calling the White House. I just mean I came away from those times thinking differently—wrongly—about myself or about God or about how I was to live my life. Those friendships influenced me in the wrong way.

Is there a friendship God may have His giant finger on, wanting you to reconsider what that relationship is doing for you? Is God the Farmer pointing out to you, His field, a rock, weed, or stump-style friendship that's an obstruction to your growth?

I've found one indicator of God wanting you to rethink a relationship is when you hear talks about friendships or even read this section, something in your stomach ties up a little, and you can't help but think—even in the back of your mind—"Uh, this reminds me of my friendship with [fill in the blank]. Yikes."

It's painful (and awkward!) to break with someone who's a close friend—especially over something as difficult to define as "hindering my growth as a human"—but, according to God's economy, something better will come from it. Something better will grow in that spot.

Now, let's talk about dating The Wrong Person. I've spent a large part of my adult life meeting with college students and single young adults. I can tell you, flat-out, dating relationships with The Wrong Person steer people further and faster from what God wants to grow in them than anything else. Period.

I've seen all-star girls—girls who had so many great things growing in their lives, with their heads screwed on straight, and with an awareness of God's love and how it's meant to affect them—get connected with The Wrong Person and (in no time, it seemed), they started acting like someone they really weren't. They settled when it came to moral principles that had once been important to them, settled on what kind of person they really wanted to be connected with, and settled on what they'd come to expect a dating relationship could actually do for them and their growth.

I've seen dudes get so captivated (and even obsessed) by some beautiful woman (usually someone they'd always imagined was out of their league), that when they start dating them, the whole relationship takes over their lives. And because the girl isn't stable, or doesn't consider God's plans for growth as important for her, or because she's only in the relationship for fun (despite the guy's more serious devotion to her), the relationship keeps the guy from growing. It even kills off some of the crops God's grown in the guy's life earlier.

To be honest, this was me with most of my dating relationships before I met Kristin. That's not a knock on those girls—it's more of a knock on me. I got into those relationships and idealized those women so much I lost sight of what was not only good for me but what was good for them. Only once I got out of those relationships did I see the *relationship* was bad for me . . . and bad for them too.

More than Wrong Person friendships, Wrong Person dating relationships are very difficult to identify when you're in the midst of them.

Imagine you're standing on a beach as a hurricane hits. Over the course of just an hour, the wind speed shoots up from fifteen miles per hour to one hundred miles per hour. With sand blowing everywhere, roofs flying off, and waves crashing over everything in sight, it'd be hard to miss that hurricane.

Now imagine you're standing on that same beach, but this time the hurricane comes in much more slowly. Imagine the wind speeds increasing only two miles per hour every hour.

You may not notice that increase at all. It's only a little blowing sand. And the waves are a touch higher. And the shingles flutter, but barely. But that's all just normal activity at the beach.

And, little by little, the winds increase and the waves get higher and the roofs get shakier, but because it's happening slowly, you hardly notice.

But anyone who happens to show up at the beach a few hours into this hurricane notices the disaster going on. Even if you don't.

We often live in denial in bad dating relationships until they completely fall apart, and we find ourselves facedown in the sand, twenty feet underwater, with a Corolla floating past us. "Um, I think I'm in a hurricane," we finally admit.

When I dated The Wrong Person and I felt like God was communicating to me that I was dating The Wrong Person, I usually responded by justifying the relationship and avoiding any conversation about it altogether.

Justification: "God, I mean, really . . . I'm helping this girl become better. And, besides, no one else is around for me to date, so why not her? And it's not like I'm a terrible person. Oh! And did you see that girl my buddy is dating? She's even wrong-er for him than this girl is for me! Not that she's wrong for me—I'm not willing to agree with You on that, yet, I'm just saying . . . She's not a terrible person, God! And please don't tell me you have 'someone better' for me! I can't keep waiting around! Be cool, God!"

Avoidance: "Uh, God, I'm not really up for talking about that relationship. Not right now. Let's talk about something else. Anything else. Like, poor people in Africa. Surely you care about them, right? And you must care about them a lot more than you care about some dude out in California and the girl he's dating. Let's change the subject. Be cool, God!"

Justification and avoidance are both pretty strong signs you're in a dating relationship with The Wrong Person.

Man, it's tough to listen to God when He communicates that you're in one of those Wrong Person dating relationships. It's even tougher to act on what He's saying. But in the end, by letting go of that kind of relationship, you get something much, much better. Again, this is my—and dozens and dozens of my friends'—personal experience.

(Note: I'm talking about *dating* The Wrong Person—not being *married* to The Wrong Person. When you're dating someone, you're not in a lifelong commitment or covenant with them. It's still a time of checking to see if this is someone you want to spend your lifetime with. Not so with a marriage. If you're in a marriage with someone who you feel is The Wrong Person, God's probably not telling you to leave them. God doesn't see the bottom portion of a marriage certificates where you sign your name as perforated. It's firmly attached. If you're seeing your spouse as The Wrong Person, get some counseling, talk to friends, and get help to keep you moving your marriage forward, not backward. God grows great things as you fight for your marriage. It's completely and unalterably true.)

LOVING YOUR HURT

According to my spellcheck and dictionary, *unforgiveness* is not an official word. How is that possible when words like *whereas* and *heretofore* and *kerfuffle* are actual words? C'mon!

For this book, *unforgiveness* shall be a real word. (Eat it, Merriam-Webster.)

It should be a real word because it accurately describes a real—and dangerous—problem.

Unforgiveness is when someone's done something to hurt us and we hold it against them.

And unforgiveness is one of the most destructive rocks, weeds, or stumps a farmer could ever find on a field.

I've known people who were hurt by someone years ago and, despite the fact the offender had apologized, they held a grudge against them. For years. Something inside them felt like, "Y'know, I get you're saying you're sorry. And you may even be sorry. But this hurt is so big and so deep that I can't let it slide. If I were to forgive you for this, it would undercut how much pain it's caused me. So in an effort to affirm my pain and reassure myself that this was a truly bad thing, I'm going to stay frustrated with you, distant with you, or angry with you."

I've known friends who are unforgiving toward their friends. Children who are unforgiving toward their parents. Parents who won't forgive their kids. Coworkers who are unforgiving toward their bosses, colleagues, and employees. Individuals who are unforgiving toward entire races or people groups. Spouses who won't forgive a husband or wife who hurt them.

Jesus talked about unforgiveness . . . a lot. But He always talked about it in the light of something else: our forgiveness.

To point out the destructiveness of unforgiveness and its root causes, Jesus uses some sound logic. He knows that in order to combat something that's wildly emotional—driven by what we feel and how we deal with those feelings—sometimes it's best to rely on a logical, orderly "argument."

Here's my take on Jesus' logical argument against unforgiveness—as though it were explained in a dialogue in a diner between Jesus and a guy named . . . I don't know . . . how about . . . Lance? They've both ordered frittatas, of course.

Jesus: (to the waitress, as she drops off His orange juice) *Thank you.*

Lance: *You know, Jesus. I'm really hurt. Like, really, really hurt.*

Jesus: *I'm sorry, Lance. I am.*

Lance: *Thanks, Jesus.*

Lance thinks some more about his hurt. And an angry look comes over his face.

Lance: *I don't even want to talk to the person who hurt me anymore. I know, I know—they hurt me a while ago. But it still hurts! And, yes, they apologized—or at least seemed to—but that doesn't offset what they did and its effect on me.*

Jesus: *Sounds like you're not willing to—*

Lance: *—forgive them? You're always talking about forgiveness. C'mon, Jesus. Let me hold onto this one, okay? Can't I be unforgiving just this once?*

Jesus: *You can, Lance.*

Lance: *Thanks, Jesus.*

Jesus: *But it's gonna destroy you.*

Lance: *I knew it. You're not going to let me just—*

Jesus: *No, I'm not. I care about you, buddy. I don't want you wallowing around in all of this. It's not right.*

Lance: *"Not right?!" What's "not right" about it? They—*

Jesus: *Can I ask you a few questions, Lance?*

Lance: *Sure, Jesus. But, if they're, like, trivia questions, you're probably going to beat me—*

Jesus: *Lance, have you ever done anything wrong in your life?*

Lance: *Well, yeah. Sure.*

Jesus: *Like, maybe, a lot of things?*

Lance: *Of course. We've talked about this before, right?*

Jesus: *We have, but I just want to make sure you get a sense of the scope of some of the wrong you've done.*

Lance: *Hang on. It's not like I held up a bank or turned off the power to a hospital or stole a bag of puppies.*

Jesus: *I know. But can we agree you've done things in your life that have hurt God? Maybe made Him sad or frustrated?*

Lance: *Yeah. I have. I mean, I know that lots of times I've just done the opposite of what He was telling me to do. I've let my temper get out of control more than a few times. I seem to get a kick out of being jealous of other people and what they have. I lust . . . a lot. I—*

Jesus: *You don't need to list it all out, man. That's not the point of this.*

Lance: *Thank God.*

Jesus: *You're welcome. Now, how does God feel about you because of all that?*

Lance: *Like, today? Right now?*

Jesus: *Yes.*

Lance: *Well, I mean, according to the Bible, y'know—*

Jesus: *I'm familiar with it.*

Lance: *Well, because I believe You walked around and lived on earth and then died as a sacrifice to get rid of my sins, God doesn't stay mad at me.*

Jesus: *Right. What's another way of saying that?*

Lance: *I'm not following you.*

Jesus: *If you believe in me, then when it comes to all you've done wrong, you are . . .*

Lance: *Oh. Forgiven.*

Jesus: *And what are you forgiven of?*

Lance: *Everything.*

Jesus: *Yes. Okay. So just to recap: you've done a fair amount of things that have hurt God—*

Lance: *I'd say more than a "fair" amount. It's been all my life, you know . . .*

Jesus: *Okay. You've done a "lot" of things that have hurt God. But even though you've done all that, God has completely and utterly forgiven you, right? Like, there's not a trace of anything you've done wrong that God hasn't forgiven, right?*

Lance: *Right.*

Jesus: *Lots of wrong, but all is forgiven. Does that sum it up?*

Lance: *Yeah.*

Jesus: *Okay. Good. Now, Lance, if you've done lots of wrong, but God has forgiven every bit of those wrongs— even though they really, truly, and deeply hurt God—then does it make sense that you'd hold one thing against someone else?*

Lance stares off, thinking.

Jesus: *Has God been unforgiving to you for all you've done to hurt Him?*

Lance: *No.*

Jesus: *Then why would you feel justified in holding onto one thing someone's done to hurt you?*

Lance: *I don't know.*

Jesus: *I'm not saying this to make you feel terrible. I'm saying this to help you see that being unforgiving while being completely forgiven is—*

Lance: *Prideful. Kind of arrogant, even.*

Jesus: *I was going to say, "illogical," but I won't argue with those either.*

Lance: *But, Jesus, I can't just forgive that person. It's not that easy.*

Jesus: *I know. It's hard. It's very hard. But, Lance, this is the first time I've actually ever heard you say anything that even remotely communicated that you wanted to even just* think *about forgiving them. I can help you forgive. But I can't step in to help you unless you ask for that help.*

Lance: *Can I ask You a question, Jesus?*

Jesus: *It's not about whether or not Adam and Eve had belly buttons, is it?*

Lance: *Why is all of this forgiveness stuff so important?*

Jesus: *Three reasons. The first has to do with the other person. You may not sense it, but you're hurting the person who hurt you by not letting them off the hook. And God doesn't like people hurting other people. Just like He didn't like it when they hurt you, He doesn't like it that you're hurting them.*

Lance: *That makes sense.*

Jesus: *And, two, bitterness. Bitterness is awful, Lance. I can't really communicate strongly enough how awful it is. It tears people apart. It ruins friendships and families and groups of Jesus followers and companies and races and countries. It even tears individuals in two. It sucks the joy out of life, fuels the fires of self-focus, and makes people less and less likely to open themselves to other people because they're so sensitive and fearful of being hurt again. Bitterness is soul cancer. It's spiritual suicide. It's terrible, Lance. Trust me. I have seen bitterness destroy humans for thousands and thousands of years. There's no upside to unforgiveness, Lance. None.*

Lance: *I see.*

Lance takes a long drink of coffee as he thinks.

Lance: *And the third reason?*

Jesus: *Because unforgiveness and the bitterness it produces makes it really, really hard for Me to grow good things in you. Things like kindness, happiness for others, contentment. Even love for yourself. I have great things in store for your life, and I want to bring them out in you, but holding things against others gums that whole process up. I plant the seeds of those good things, but unforgiveness chokes the plants out. The crop never comes.*

Lance: *So, You mean, I'm like a field or something, and You're like a farmer?*

Jesus: *Oh, good. You've been paying attention to the book so far.*

Their frittatas arrive. Jesus suddenly puts his finger on his nose.

Lance: *What are you doing?*

Jesus: *Last to touch their nose has to pray.*

Lance: *Nice, Jesus.*

We all have a natural tendency to hold our hurts close to us, seeing them as so powerful they have more control over us than we have over how we respond to them.

Is there someone in your life you're not forgiving? Maybe they've asked for your forgiveness. Maybe they've begged for it. Maybe they haven't asked for it. Maybe they don't even know they hurt you. Maybe they don't care.

Or maybe, like me, you have a tendency to overlook big hurts, getting hung up on the smaller, daily ones instead.

One of my favorite movies is called *The Tree of Life*. This movie isn't for everyone. It doesn't have much of a discernible plot. It's like watching a two-hour poem (with Brad Pitt and Sean Penn playing out parts of the poem) that's about God and people and suffering and hope.

In the opening voice-over, the main character describes the fight within each of us—

> The nuns taught us there are two ways through life: the way of nature and the way of grace. You have to choose which one you'll follow.
>
> Grace doesn't try to please itself. Accepts being slighted, forgotten, disliked. Accepts insults and injuries.
>
> Nature only wants to please itself. Get others to please it too. Likes to lord it over them. To have its own way. It finds reasons to be unhappy when all the world is shining around it, when love is smiling through all things.

All too often, I give in to the way of nature. I hold onto offenses, find reasons to be unhappy, and let bitterness and frustration overtake me. When my wife doesn't do something for me I'd like her to do, I let nature tell me she doesn't really care about me that much. And I hold it against her. It's not about being

---

unforgiving toward a massive hurt—it's more about allowing a long series of small offenses to pile up.

Which weighs more? A single, one-ton brick or a pile of two thousand one-pound bricks?

Being unforgiving for one big hurt isn't that different from allowing a thousand little hurts to go unforgiven.

That's my tendency. A thousand hurts going unforgiven.

I don't want that, though.

Why? Because I want the good stuff God wants to grow in me more than I want to hold on to my hurts. I'd rather experience the world shining around me and love smiling through all things.

I want to love all that stuff more than I seem to love my hurt. I want to let go and forgive and extend grace and find grace and, through all of that, receive the good things God has for me.

I also want to receive God's forgiveness more and more in my own life. (Jesus says in Matthew 6:15 that if I don't forgive others, God won't forgive me. Uh, yikes.)

I want to let God get rid of that unforgiveness weed, rock, or stump. I want something better in exchange for it.

Don't you?

BAD PRESCRIPTION

When I was a kid, I thought it was hilarious to put on my dad's eyeglasses and walk around the house. After a while, though, I'd start bumping into things because my depth perception was off, and I'd get a level of headache known only to hockey players who refuse to wear helmets.

Those glasses distorted my view of reality and caused me pain. Eventually, even though it was fun to wear them, I realized I had to take them off.

92

Those glasses are like bad mindsets. A mindset is a way of looking at and interpreting the world, other people, God, and ourselves. A good mindset is calibrated according to whatever is true. A bad mindset is calibrated according to whatever is false.

My dad's old glasses weren't calibrated to give me a correct view of the world. Things close up looked far away, and things far away looked like they'd been stretched out, like Silly Putty. Sizes and distances were impossible to reckon correctly as the whole world seemed to throb whenever I turned my head, like I was stuck in a Dalí painting.

Bad mindsets do the same to us, just on a deeper level. We look at the world and misjudge what's going on, how people are truly responding to us, and how we're meant to read our own thoughts and emotions. They give us a distorted view of things and cause us to trip and flounder while also causing us pain.

Bad mindsets are some of the biggest obstructions to God growing something good in me.

I was a devoted David Letterman fan all through middle school, high school, and college. His I-really-couldn't-care-less-about-what's-going-on-here attitude mixed with an isn't-this-world-ridiculous-so-why-take-anything-truly-serious outlook tickled me.

Letterman was a world-class insult assassin too—able to knock any puffed-up, self-important movie stars down a few pegs with a well-worded jab. But what few people picked up on at the time was Letterman saved his best insults for himself.

Something inside that guy from Indianapolis seemed to have it in for that guy from Indianapolis. When he made a mistake during the show, he'd run himself down right away, in front of the entire viewing audience. He consistently made fun of his hair and his teeth and his awkwardness and his introversion. He seemed to love telling stories about when he was slighted by someone else, squarely placing the blame for the interaction on himself.

I have a feeling Letterman gravitated toward verbal self-immolation because he knew if he made fun of himself first—beating anyone else to the punch—then they couldn't make fun of him.

Over time I came to adopt that attitude too.

I'm not blaming David Letterman for my tendencies, by the way. I want to say for the record: "Dave, this isn't on you! Not in a million years! Love you, buddy. And thanks for reading my book."

For years I made a hobby out of making fun of myself before other people could. It was some weird social defense mechanism that fired up during my I'm-awkward-and-I'm-sure-other-people-think-I'm-awkward high school years. It was designed to take the insult out of other people's mouths before they could deliver it themselves. I didn't want anyone to think for a moment I was oblivious to some defect in my style, looks, personality, or character. So my plan was to make fun of me before they could.

In ninth grade I had a pair of shorts with some crazy pattern on them. I wore them to some summer picnic thing and a buddy of mine was there. The kid didn't even have a chance to look at the shorts before I started telling him how ugly they were. "You can laugh at them, if you want," I said. (I'm sure the kid was thinking, "Uh, dude? I haven't noticed your shorts and really don't care about your shorts.")

This type of behavior lasted for a couple of decades.

Then a few years ago, God started talking with me about that tendency. "Why are you talking about yourself like this? Why do you even see yourself this way? And, further, why do you think other people in your life are automatically thinking insulting, critical things about you?"

This mindset, God was saying, was destructive, causing me to see the world incorrectly and also causing me pain. Not unlike those old glasses.

So God asked me to start being aware when I was about to say something insulting about myself and to hold back.

The process started with me noticing when I was about to run myself down. Usually, I'd go ahead and say the thing (because I thought it was really true, needed to be said, or was kind of funny), but at least I'd noticed my pattern. Then over time I began to try to cut out one or two of those insults here and there.

This change wasn't easy. That verbal self-destruction habit was ingrained in me. I realized I'd come to believe self-deprecation was a part of my personality, and if it was gone, then how could I possibly appropriately interact with other people?

My friend Mike called this behavior out in me. He said my tendency to "talk crap" about myself had reached monumental proportions. He recognized it was destroying me from the inside out.

Then I started to see it more clearly. I saw I'd become delusional about the whole self-deprecation thing. It was sad, really. I began to realize too that seeing myself this way didn't just extend to myself and to how others saw me—it affected how I thought God saw me. I genuinely thought God didn't like me as much as I (and, assumedly, others) didn't like me.

So over time I've worked at it. I'm happy to say I'm much better at avoiding those comments. God's prompted me whenever I've been about to say anything self-derogatory, and He's helped me to say something else.

(I still struggle, though. No kidding: just as I wrote this, someone emailed me an old photo of myself. I immediately wrote back a scathing—but kind of funny—comment about how terrible I looked. Old habits die hard.)

The results have been great. One of them is that my wife seems to have a little more respect for me. If I'm constantly walking around talking about what a loser I am, how can I possibly expect that she'd naturally form a positive opinion about me?

When I quit verbalizing negative things about myself, it became easier to stop thinking of myself that way. And as I've come to think less negatively about myself, I get a better sense of the progress God's made—and is making in me—and I feel more hopeful about the future.

From the outside, that bad mindset may have seemed like a small weed, rock, or stump. But God saw it differently. He knew it had to be removed. That process wasn't easy—it was painful even. But by removing it, God's been able to grow good fruit in me. He's grown optimism, more confidence, and hope. And these things haven't just made my life better, but (I believe) God has used those things to benefit people I'm in relationship with as well.

The lenses you use to see yourself, your spouse, your friends, your coworkers, people in your community, and God dictate how you'll respond to life. If those lenses are the wrong prescription, the best thing you can do is trust God when He asks you to dump them so He can give you the right lenses— and all of the good things that come along with seeing the world the way He sees the world. You'll give up something that produces death in order to gain more of life.

THE BETTER END OF THE DEAL

Sometimes I'll catch our younger daughter Bomber walking around while holding a fork. Not a plastic kid fork, mind you. No. Like a big, metal, adult, mini-trident fork. Now, this child has a bazillion actual, made-for-children toys, but for some reason, in that moment, it's very important for her to walk around with big metal fork in her hand, tines pointed up at her face.

As a good dad, I kneel down, look her in the eye and say, "Now, I don't want you to get all upset, so I'm going to let you run around in circles wearing your socks on the slippery tile floor while you hold that fork. Who am I to disagree with what makes you happy? Enjoy, honey."

No!

I kneel down and go, "Sweetie, that is very, very dangerous. I don't want you to slip and fall and hurt yourself. I'm going to lift you up and you can drop it right in the sink, and it'll make a fun, loud clanking noise. But then we're going to go play with something else. Okay?"

Sometimes Bomber goes along with this, and sometimes she doesn't, but in either case, I'm trying to get rid of the destructive thing to give her something better.

In Bomber's case, she rarely has an option with this switch. She's a little kid, and her brain doesn't get that fork = danger. He brain thinks, fork = fun! But I'm older and taller and smarter than her—and I also love her a bunch—so, since fork = danger, we have to get rid of the fork. Sometimes she hands it over, and sometimes I have to take it from her.

Most of the time God seems inclined to give us the option about when we'll allow Him to deal with weeds, rocks, and stumps. He rarely forces us into forgiveness, makes us change our mindset, or removes destructive relationships from our lives without our say-so. Sometimes He does . . . but that doesn't seem like His normal way of doing business. Instead He comes to us and asks if it's okay for Him to remove it.

And when the removal of that obstruction causes us pain . . . He hurts too.

I've taken forks and other dangerous items away from my daughter, and when she wails about it, I don't laugh at her and walk away. I comfort her, hug her, and try to communicate to her why I did what I did. Sometimes she receives all of that, sometimes she doesn't. But I know my job is to love her in that pain—even though I know removing the fork was the best thing for her.

God's the same way with us. I believe that. When you trust Him—acting on your belief He's completely wise and totally loving—and you give up that destructive dating relationship—and it makes you hurt and you cry—God is there. When you feel as though you're betraying yourself and your hurt when you finally choose forgiveness—God is there. When you let Him rewire your thinking and it causes you to wonder if you're losing a core part of yourself—God is there. He doesn't abandon us during—or after—the obstruction removal process. He comes to us. He comforts us.

He also reminds us: "What you've allowed me to do—though it hurts right now—is ultimately good."

Frederick Buechner says it like this: "What's lost is nothing to what's found, and all the death there ever was, set next to life, would scarcely fill a cup."

_____

Jim Elliot was a guy back in the 1940s and 1950s who had everything going for him. He was an incredibly good-looking, intelligent, charismatic dude. When you read about this guy, you picture him going on to run a massive company or becoming president or starring in movies. But during college, Jim discovered a deep passion for Jesus, so instead of pursuing fame or wealth or power, in 1952, along with some Jesus-following friends, Jim headed down to Ecuador to tell people that Jesus is great and really loves the Ecuadorians.

A mere four years later, Jim and his friends were killed in Ecuador by the very people they'd gone to love.

Jim's story is strange and heartbreaking. But it's also, somehow, inspiring and moving. His story can be summed up in a quote that he's become famous for: "He is no fool who gives what he cannot keep to gain that which he cannot lose."

For Jim, giving up the seemingly amazing opportunities for his own success in America wasn't worth what God would bring his way if he trusted Him and gave his life to the purposes God had in mind.

And even though he died at a young age, I firmly believe (as did his widow, Elisabeth Elliot) Jim would look back at the "trade" he made and believe he got the better end of the deal.

We'll never be fools if we give up something of limited value—

—unforgiveness, a destructive friendship, the wrong dating relationship, a bad way of looking at ourselves or others—

—to get something that's even better—

—good fruit like love, joy, peace, patience, kindness, goodness, gentleness, self-control, mercy, a better relationship, a lasting marriage, a heart at rest, a view of the world more in line with God's grace.

Three Questions

What's one obstruction you think God may want to remove in your life?

What keeps you from letting Him remove it?

If that obstruction was gone, how could your life—or the lives of people around you—improve?

Chapter 5
The Seed

Then the word of the LORD came to [Elijah].

—1 Kings 17:8

The Farmer opens the barn door. Sunlight floods in. He walks toward the back—toward rows of burlap sacks, bursting at the seams. He kneels down and, with the excitement of a child, opens one. He pushes his hand down into the sack's contents, letting his fingers wiggle and weave amongst the thousands and thousands of dried, dark kernels of corn.

He pulls one kernel out, holding it up to the light, admiring it.

Such a small thing—no more than a quarter of an inch long—yet the Farmer knows that given the right amount of sun, water, and care, and if planted in the right spot at the right time, the seemingly insignificant bit of organic matter will grow into a stalk as tall as ten feet and burst with ears of corn as big as his forearm.

The seed will transform into something four or five hundred times larger.

From a bag farther down the line, the Farmer removes a wheat seed. It's even smaller than the corn kernel. Eventually, this seed will become a wheat stalk standing four feet tall. Even more impressive about this seed is that it holds the promise of bread—the world's food staple. Staring at the seed, he imagines a piping hot loaf of bread emerging from an oven. Quietly, to himself, he says, "Who'd imagine something like that could come from something like this?"

Beyond the burlap bags, a line of small, green bushes sits on the barn floor. The nondescript and unimpressive bushes look like average, leafy greenery that might line the side of the house to cover damaged brick—but these are anything but ordinary. The Farmer can see in them what they'll soon produce once they've been planted in the field, watered just right, and soaked in the sun: gorgeous white, red, and pink roses. From something ordinary will come something extraordinary.

The Farmer surveys the bags of seeds and the huddle of bushes. Sitting there, on the barn floor, they don't look like much. But to the Farmer, they're all important and precious. Each tiny kernel and each delicate plant represent what will soon come forth from them.

Those seeds are the first stages of growth, leading to a variety of glorious crops.

He can't wait to bring the seed to the field.

LET US MARVEL

Before we get into what those seeds represent, it would be good to pause for a moment and marvel. Yes, I said, "marvel." That's something we don't do much these days. We take for granted things that should be making us marvel—be filled with wonder and astonishment to such a degree that our mouths drop open a little and we say things like, "Well I'll be . . ." or "This is one of the most amazing things I've ever seen in my life" or "I'm gobsmacked. Surely I am." When was the last time you looked at the phone you keep in your pocket—the device that can let you look up almost any piece of data in the world and play almost any piece of recorded music ever and functions as the video phone the Jetsons promised us decades ago—and truly marveled? Or air travel—flying through the sky in a giant tennis ball can with wings, taking a hundred weary travelers from Omaha to O'Hare? Or your microwave—the thing that heats up burritos to surface-of-Venus level temperatures using nuclear radiation and space rays (or something like that)?

When was the last time you marveled at plant growth? I know: it's not as technologically sexy as a new iPhone or a microwave that can pop a marshmallow in four seconds flat. We probably don't marvel at plant growth because we've become used to it. It's woven into the fabric of our world—it's how most food comes about. It's something we were shown when we were little kids and, since then, we've just taken it for granted.

But this is an incredible, wild, marvelous process!

You take a teeny tiny seed, you put it in the ground, you add water and sunlight, and then—voilà!—you have something much, much bigger and more useful (and more delicious, usually) than that original seed.

That is crazy!

Seriously. Stop for a moment. Sit where you're sitting or stand where you're standing. (Wait, why are you standing while reading a book?) And just think. Think about that process. Think about how impressive it is. Think about how miraculous it is.

Marvel at it.

(Come back here when you're done with your marvel session.)

Why am I having you marvel at this? Because if you don't see that the transition from itty-bitty seed to big, delicious crop isn't mind-blowing, you won't have the right level of expectation for what God wants to do in you by planting a seed and growing it into something bigger and more useful.

The transformation that's meant to happen in your life isn't supposed to be small, unremarkable, or shrug inducing. It's meant to be remarkable. It's meant to stop you (and the people around you) in their tracks. It's meant to be marvelous.

So with that level of hope and expectation and excitement, let's look at the seed.

THE GREAT STEAK DECREE

You don't have to have grown up in Iowa to know that a field won't grow anything without seed. You don't look at an apple tree and wonder, "Where did that come from?" You know that, at some point, an apple seed fell down on that spot and, after a lot of water, sun, and time, that big ol' apple tree emerged. Having learned about Johnny Appleseed in second grade is really all the agricultural training you need to get this point.

So what does the seed represent in our metaphor? What is that little thing that can go from seemingly insignificant to something "as high as an elephant's eye" (as they describe corn in the song from the musical *Oklahoma!* my daughters have come to love)?

The seed is the word of God.

"The word of God" is kind of a weird phrase, isn't it? It sounds so formal and even daunting. But since it's found all throughout the Bible, it's not just a phrase we can blow off. Here's just a handful of examples:

> After this, the word of the LORD came to Abram.
>
> —Genesis 15:1

> The word of the LORD came to Solomon.
>
> —1 Kings 6:11

Then the word of the LORD came to Elijah.

—1 Kings 17:2

Peter remembered the word the LORD had spoken to him.

—Luke 22:61

So what is "the word of the Lord"?

Imagine I go to a fancy steakhouse known for big, tasty cuts of marbleized meat. When the waiter comes to my table, I say: "My name is Jeff Davenport. I'm glad to be eating here. I'd like to tell you what I want to eat. I'm going to begin with the beet and kale salad." (This is a completely fictional story as there is no way in this world I would ever willingly eat either beets or kale. These are the devil's vegetables.)

The waiter nods and writes down my salad order. Then I say, "For my main dish, I'd like a baked potato and the porterhouse. Now, I'd like that steak done medium-well. That means just the slightest bit of pink, right in the center. I decree this. Make sense—" (I read his name tag) "—Earl?"

Earl the Waiter nods. "Yes, sir."

Earl goes back to the chef and probably says something like, "I need a gross salad, a baked potato, and a medium-well steak for the weirdo at table 23."

Instead, imagine Earl says this: "The word of Jeff Davenport has come to me. It has informed me he'd like that one salad no one really likes but keeps ordering, a baked potato, and the porterhouse with barely a trace of pink. This is the word of Jeff Davenport to I, Earl the Waiter."

In this case "the word of Jeff Davenport" is whatever I have communicated to someone else.

To demystify it, that's all the word of God really is: whatever God has communicated to someone or a group of someones.

In the Bible, sometimes the word of God is a wise statement. Sometimes it's a direction for a person, a family, or a community. Sometimes it's an expression of God's opinion on a matter. In any case, the word of God is God speaking truth.

So in our metaphor, the seed is the word of God that He's communicating . . . to you.

Jesus explicitly made the seed = the word of God connection when He was teaching a group of folks out by a lake. He told them an extended metaphor about a guy who wanted to grow things. It began with:

"A farmer went out to sow his seed" (Luke 8:5).

Then Jesus told about where the seed fell and what ended up happening to it. (More about this in the next chapter.)

He ended the metaphor with a great punch line about the seed that fell on good soil.

"It came up and yielded a crop, a hundred times more than was sown" (v. 8).

Jesus explained to His closest buddies that the seed represented what God had to say to the people. It represented His insights or His truth. And if people received those insights and truth, a bountiful crop would rise up.

For God to grow good things in our lives—things that can radically impact ourselves and the people around us—He has to plant seeds. And those seeds are ideas, concepts, directions—truths—He's communicating specifically to us. Without those seeds, nothing grows.

So how does God communicate the word of the Lord to us? He does it through the Holy Spirit.

I know when many Jesus followers think of the Holy Spirit, they imagine some mysterious form that's doing wild and woolly things we just don't understand. Well, let's take a bit of the fear of the unknown about the Holy Spirit and say that one of the things the Holy Spirit does is tell us what God is thinking. (See 1 Corinthians 2 for more on this.)

So if we'll stop and listen to the Holy Spirit, we can actually get a sense of God's thoughts about us. In other words, His word.

Now this of course leads to another question: "Okay, man. If God wants to communicate His word to me through His Holy Spirit, how does *that* happen?"

Glad you asked. I believe He does it in four main ways . . .

#1: THE BIBLE

If you've been a Jesus follower for long at all, you've probably heard the Bible referred to as God's Word. That's a pretty good descriptor but maybe a better nickname for it is, "Things God has said to people."

The big, giant book (Honestly, isn't it the biggest book in your house that's not written by Tom Clancy, David Foster Wallace, or a nineteenth-century Russian?) is full of stories when God communicated, via a variety of means, to a variety of people.

It's also full of wisdom for life. These are things that are true for anybody and everybody who's living on earth. The Book of Proverbs is full of this good stuff. Same with Ecclesiastes.

The Bible is, really, a big book of truth. It's the book God guided humans to write so He could get His truth out in the world in a way that's accessible to humans. And we know that what God communicates is truth because, first, He's completely wise (He sees it all and knows it all) and, second, He's not a liar (why would God lie? He's not trying to get out of going to school or convince you He didn't drink the last of milk and then put the empty carton back in the fridge).

Because the Bible is objectively true, we can use it as a standard to hold more subjective ways of finding out the word of God (numbers 2–4 in this list) up to. It's like a truth ruler. Anything can be measured against it to find out if it's actually true.

So how does the word of God come to us through the Bible?

I can tell you from my own personal experience that it comes in one of two ways:

1. "Oh, yeah. That makes sense."
2. "Okay, this is weird, but when I read that, I got this crazy . . . feeling . . . or something."

The first way is pretty straightforward.

I've struggled with being lazy most of my life. I'm sure there are a dozen psychological reasons for this (fear of failure, past hurt, a desire to watch twelve hours of TV rather than do something productive), but the point is it's easy for me to disengage from *doing* in favor of . . . *not doing*.

One day I was reading the Bible. It was a part in Proverbs where God uses a pretty clear metaphor to describe hard workers. It goes like this:

> Go to the ant, you sluggard; consider its ways and be wise! It has no commander, no overseer or ruler, yet it stores its provisions in summer and gathers its food at harvest. How long will you lie there, you sluggard? When will you get up from your sleep? A little sleep, a little slumber, a little folding of the hands to rest—and poverty will come on you like a thief and scarcity like an armed man.
>
> —Proverbs 6:6–11

That may seem kind of harsh to you, but it didn't seem harsh to me when I read it. Something in me went, "Oh, yes. I am being lazy. And if I'm lazy now, I can't complain six months from now if I haven't achieved the goals I've imagined myself achieving. Work now; enjoy later."

That's a pretty sensible response to that bit of truth, right? It probably doesn't seem like any sort of supernatural, close encounter with God, yet it still had its intended effect: it made me see myself differently and aim to make decisions for long-term gain rather than short-term pleasure.

I read something in the Bible. It made sense to me. It seemed to connect with something in my life. I decided it was probably something God wanted to communicate to me.

That's how the seed—the word of God—got into my field.

The other way of receiving seed from the Bible isn't so logical.

A few months ago, I was reading a big story in the Old Testament about God's chosen people—the Israelites—and how God was guiding them. At the time, God was using a guy named Joshua to show the folks where to go.

I was reading along, minding my own business, hitting sentences like:

So and so was from this one tribe, and then this other guy was from this other tribe, and then they all went to this unpronounceable city to face off against the Somethingites...

Then I hit a sentence that made me stop.

> Be very careful to keep the commandment and the law that Moses the servant of the Lord gave you: to love the Lord your God, to walk in obedience to him, to keep his commands, to hold fast to him and to serve him with all your heart and with all your soul.
>
> —Joshua 22:5

Now there's a lot in there, but one particular part jumped out at me:

Hold fast.

It reminded me of a fact I'd recently learned about sailors in the old days. When massive storms would come, sailors would lash themselves to the mast (tie themselves to the big stick in the middle of the boat that held the sail) so when the wind and waves came, they wouldn't get knocked overboard.

It also reminded me of an image from a movie I love: *Master and Commander: The Far Side of the World*. In it, an old, salty sea dog onboard a nineteenth-century warship shows the letters tattooed across his knuckles to a young boy. The letters read HOLD FAST. The old sailor uses the phrase to communicate to the boy the secret of survival at sea.

When I read that phrase, "hold fast," in the Bible, it didn't fully make sense to me like the passage about the ants had. It struck me in a different way. It was less about logic and more about something stirring in my bones—in my soul. It's hard to articulate how it felt, but I just know that it felt as though something were communicating with me—something besides the logic board in my brain.

I had this *impression* God was telling me, "Jeff, it's good to hold fast . . . to Me." I believe that was Him speaking through His Holy Spirit.

It was as though God was saying, "Jeff, even though that section of the Bible was written for the Israelites thousands of years ago, it's for you too. Hold fast to Me. Don't hold fast to your efforts. Don't hold fast to luck. Don't hold fast to nice thoughts. Hold fast to Me."

That was God's word for me: *hold fast.*

That was the seed God wanted to plant inside of me.

#2: TEACHERS

Teachers are really just anybody who you go and listen to as they talk about God and what He's saying—primarily via the Bible. On many Sunday mornings, my wife and I go and hear two different teachers teach at a local church place. Many times, when I'm flying on an airplane, I'll listen to a podcast of a teacher I like who lives in New York City teach about God and the Bible. I even consider lots of authors I like to be teachers in this vein because they teach me what God might be saying. I say a teacher is worth listening to if they are following Jesus, believe in God's truth, and seem to actually love the people they're teaching.

Recently I was listening to a teacher talk about Jesus and siblings Mary, Martha, and Lazarus, as recorded in John 11. I've heard the story of Jesus raising Lazarus from the dead a hundred times; so, honestly, I was kind of tuned out. But then, suddenly, the teacher person said something that caught my ear. He was talking about how the Bible says, "Now Jesus loved Martha and her sister and Lazarus. So when he heard that Lazarus was sick, he stayed where he was two more days" (v. 6). The teacher guy implied it was *because* Jesus loved the two women that He waited to come to them in their distress.

Wait, what? That didn't make any sense to me. So I looked up from my phone (I was doing a digital crossword while I was semi-listening) to figure out what in the world this guy was saying.

He explained that sometimes God allows suffering in people's lives because He loves us—so He can grow us in faith.

I'd never heard that idea communicated as clearly as that guy communicated it. So instead of looking back down at my phone, I stared off and considered what he'd said.

It hit me hard because at the time I was going through a not-fun season. I'd even call it a season of suffering. Then, in that moment, I felt in my gut something akin to God saying, "Hey, Jeff. When you suffer, it's not right to think I don't love you. Please don't think that. Maybe sometimes I'm waiting to relieve your suffering because I love you and want to grow you."

Whoa.

Right then, on that Sunday morning, I felt God communicate His word to me. He told me what He was thinking about me and my circumstances, right then and there. He planted a seed in me through what the teacher guy said.

#3: OTHERS

Others is a weird way of wording what I mostly mean to be friends.

There's some bad God-belief out there that goes something like this:

"God only wants to communicate His thoughts to you through the Bible and through teacher-people. Any other means are dicey. Avoid them."

That's just not right. How do I know that? Because A) all throughout the Bible, God spoke through His people to other people to let them know what He was thinking and B) I've had plenty of experiences where God communicated to me through other people.

Let me tell you about my friend Andrew. Andrew really loves Jesus. He's been following Jesus for a long, long time. Andrew and I have been friends for about thirteen years now, and for six months we shared an apartment. We laugh a lot, love to talk about movies, think Jesus is great, and think that dead religion—just doing religious activities without pursuing relationship with God—is, well, dead. Andrew and I connect really, really well.

I trust Andrew. I've seen how he's followed Jesus for over a decade, and I respect how he views God and how he takes risks to act on his faith that God is both wise and loving. Because of this, when Andrew talks to me about my life, I pay attention.

Not long ago, Andrew and I were drinking coffee in a funky Denver coffee shop. We got to talking about our lives, and I told him a frustration I'd been having with God lately. The dialogue went something like this:

Jeff: *I really have trouble figuring God out. I mean, I'll think God is one way—He's X. Then, I'll find out He's actually a totally opposite way. He's Y. So, if I think He's X, He's Y, and if I think He's Y, He's X. Which is He?*

Andrew laughs.

Jeff: (now not just frustrated at God but frustrated at Andrew too) *What?*

Andrew: (still laughing) *I don't know, man. Maybe He just wants you to know He's mysterious sometimes and that you can't totally figure Him out.*

That wasn't what I wanted to hear. I wanted the conversation to play out like this:

Jeff: *So which is He?*

Andrew: *Y. God is Y.*

Jeff: *Thanks.*

Andrew: *No problem. More coffee?*

Jeff: *Sure.*

But it didn't. Instead Andrew told me something I didn't *want* to hear. But once he said it, I knew it was something I *needed* to hear.

There's often a big difference between what we want and what we need.

In that moment, the idea God is mysterious and it's good for me to remember that was God's word to me. It was a good seed.

I also trust my pal Steven to help me get what God's communicating to me. I've known Steven since the end of high school. I've always admired Steven's faith and his willingness to do *anything* for Jesus. Steven is wise and knows how to articulate truth.

A number of years ago, Steven was in from out of town visiting my wife and me. At one point during the weekend, Steven said rather ominously, "Hey, I'd like to sit down and talk with you two while I'm here."

We know and trust Steven, and though we were a little trepidatious, we made time to listen to him.

Steven started the conversation with this: "I'm a little nervous." (This was odd because my friend Steven is the most confident person I've ever met, hands down.) He followed this up with, "And after I tell you both what I feel like I need to tell you, you may not want to be friends with me anymore."

This, by the way, is a fantastic way to scare the heck out of anyone you're about to talk with.

Still, we knew Steven loved us and that he was very wise and whatever he had to say to us—though possibly painful— was going to be good for us.

Kristin and I both gave him the go-ahead.

Steven told us he'd recognized a bad pattern in our marriage. A pattern where we were putting other things—things that were very important and very pressing—ahead of our marriage. He recognized that, in the short term, this prioritization made sense, but in the long term, it was going to hurt us as a couple.

This was a tense subject, obviously. Basically here was a guy who was peering into our marriage and pointing out something we hadn't asked his opinion about. He was just offering it up.

But it was Steven. And we love Steven and trust Steven and know he loves us and sees a lot of things clearly. So we heard him out.

Afterwards we told him, "Thanks. Thanks for pointing out something difficult and something we had a blind spot toward." My wife was particularly open and welcoming to what he had to say.

That conversation marked a turning point for our marriage. It helped us reset some faulty prioritization and focus on putting our marriage first, even in the face of big, big issues.

Everything Steven said jibed with the Bible. I'm pretty sure he even quoted some verses. The opinion he expressed wasn't just out of thin air.

God used Steven to tell us what He was thinking. He communicated His word to us through Steven. Through Steven, He planted a seed in us.

My friend Greg is a "faith guy." He's one of the funniest, most gregarious, life-of-the-party guys you'll ever meet. He's Mr. Adventure—up for any physical challenge, any time of the day, any day of the week. That spirit feeds into how he sees God. He just plain believes God and believes God does great things, all the time, if we just trust Him and believe He's good.

Because of this, Greg has a treasure trove of stories about God doing crazy things in his life. To some people, Greg seems like an insane, wild man. But to me—and anyone else who knows Greg well—he's a "faith guy." And Greg loves reminding me of the surprising joy that's found in living by faith and trusting God in every situation. Why does he do this? Because Greg gives a rip about me. And I can sense that when he's encouraging me to live by faith.

My pal Jeeva has helped me for over a decade by consistently bringing me back to the idea that I'm a loved child of God. If he sees me living in a way that's not indicative of that, I know because he gets this look on his face and something in him gets going and he can't wait to tell me, "Dude, that's not how God sees you," or, "You need to be living out your sonship better." When he does this, he lets me know God wants me to know something: I'm a loved kid, and I need to respond to life and make decisions based on that.

My friends help me hear God's word for me—and they do it in a way that makes me feel cared about and loved.

Now, whenever I talk about listening to other people to get a sense of what God may be saying, I always need to add the following caveat:

People are humans. Even really wise and really godly people are humans. They don't get everything right all of the time. They can mishear what God may be saying, rely on their own thoughts and opinions, push a personal agenda, and be just plain wrong.

That happens.

But we can't let a fear of someone saying the wrong thing cause us to dump thinking that God can (and wants to!) speak to us through other people altogether. That's not wise at all.

#4: YOU

I ended #3 with a caveat; let me begin #4 with a caveat.

Question: *Who's the most deceptive person you know?*

Answer: *Probably you.*

I hope that doesn't sound insulting. I mean, *I'm* the most duplicitous person *I* know.

This deception and duplicity, though, isn't usually directed at other people—it's directed at ourselves.

Who fools me the most? Not other people. I fool me the most.

I come up with justifications for bad behavior, convince myself I know what I'm doing—even though I don't really—and I tell myself I've got it all under control.

So when I say, "Hey! One of the ways you can know what God is saying to you is just to sit and consider inside yourself what He may be saying," a red flag is probably coming up in you because you're thinking, "Wait. I lie to me all of the time. I have a feeling I could lie to myself about what God is saying to me. Like, I could totally convince myself that God is telling me to eat an entire box of Oreos because, in fact, I really just plain want to eat an entire box of Oreos."

We also have lots of anecdotal evidence that this I-can-hear-from-God-myself thing can go rather badly.

Think of the cult leader who has convinced himself he's Jesus' younger brother, Herb, come to save the world from sin, destruction, and bad grammar.

Or the lady who goes ballistic, shooting up a Forever 21 because "God said to."

Or the guy who says, "God told me you're supposed to marry me even though we've never met—by the way my name's Arnie—"

So instead of thinking we can hear God ourselves, we shut ourselves off to the whole endeavor. (This, by the way, is a common reason people avoid thinking about the concept of the Holy Spirit.)

But let's keep a couple of things in mind. Those statements above (the cult leader, the violent woman, Arnie) are nutty statements. Why? Because—

1. They don't match up with what God says in Scripture.
2. They probably weren't vetted by other people actively following Jesus.
3. They don't grow into something good.

I was talking with my buddy Jason recently. He told me about a dark time in his life when he felt as though God was telling him destructive things about himself. But here's the thing: Jason found all sorts of Bible verses he read in a way that seemed to affirm these destructive things. Not only that, but when he'd ask friends for their opinions about those thoughts, he'd misinterpret what they were saying, solidifying his agreement with those thoughts. It was bad all around.

One of the things that finally broke those thoughts apart happened when he was talking with a wise, older teacher-guy. Jason said to the teacher-guy, "Hey, teacher-guy, I hear you telling me a lot of good, hopeful stuff—but it seems to fly right in the face of these thoughts I've been having. What do you think?"

The wise teacher-guy stopped, got quiet for a long moment, and then said something similar to something Jesus said, "Are those thoughts growing any good fruit in you?"

Jason thought about this. Those thoughts had done nothing but drive him crazy, make him hate himself, distance himself from God and his friends, and bring him to the brink of suicide. "No," he said to the wise teacher-guy.

The wise teacher-guy then said, "Then those thoughts aren't from God."

So as we talk about listening for God's word for ourselves, let's remember it has to line up with the Bible, needs to be vetted by pals, and must make your life more fruitful—growing good things.

End of caveat.

Now how do we know that hearing God's word directly for ourselves is a valid form of communication?

Well, all throughout the Bible, God talks to people personally. Here are a few examples:

- God told Adam it wasn't good for him to be alone.
- God told Abram he was going to have a son, even though he was old.
- God told Moses to set the Israelites free from Egypt via a voice in a burning bush.
- God told Joshua to be strong and courageous.
- God told King David that someone from his family would be on the throne forever and ever.
- God told Isaiah the nation of Israel would go through a period of suffering.
- God talked to people while He was walking around the earth as Jesus.
- God told Paul to go to certain places and not go other places.
- God told Peter to be kind to people he didn't want to be kind to.
- God told John what the future would be like.

There's clear precedent for God communicating directly to people.

What does this typically look like for us nowadays?

As I said earlier, a lot of times God communicates directly to us through the Bible. Or through teachers. Or friends.

Sometimes, though, God communicates to us when we're not reading the Bible. Or when it's not Sunday morning at 9:37 a.m. Or when we're alone.

It's hard to describe what this communication feels like. As I said earlier, it's more of an impression. But these impressions usually feel like something beyond ourselves, something that's not our brain coming up with a straightforward, logical conclusion.

In my life, God has communicated directly to me things like:

It'd be good for you to give the twenty-dollar-bill you have in your wallet to a guy asking for money on the side of the road.

It's time to leave California and go and live somewhere else.

That's the girl you're going to marry.

God loves you more than you know and more than your sin should allow.

It wasn't the best idea for you to be dating that one girl.

It's not good to be unkind to yourself.

You can love your wife better by backing off on criticizing her.

If you'll be more patient when you're with your daughters, you'll enjoy parenting them so much more.

Some of these God-communiqués seemed to come to me out of the blue—like when I felt like God was letting me know it was time to leave California. And other times they came to me over a longer period of time—like hearing someone calling your name while you're asleep . . . you hear it faintly at first, but then you hear it a little more loudly, then a little more loudly, until it wakes you up. Some of them came because I'd looked at the circumstances and situations in my life, connected some dots, and realized, "I think God is trying to tell me something through all of this."

God communicating directly to me has never been clear-cut, though. God hardly ever just says something to me—without Him also saying it in another way through the Bible, a teacher/author, or a friend. It's usually a stew of communication that all lines up with a single message.

I made sure, though, that all of those God's-messages-to-Jeff met the two criteria: they matched up with what was said in the Bible and my God-loving pals agreed they sounded like they were from God.

Reading the Bible, it's clear God's big on giving money to the poor. And being kind—to others and to yourself. He also seems to like patience. Those things are all in there.

Of course, the Bible doesn't have any verses about Kristin Buzzell and whether Jeff Davenport should marry her. And there isn't a chapter describing the evils of California and how someone there should "get thee out of Dodge."

But I checked out all of those those I-can't-find-this-in-the-Bible communications with my close Jesus-following, wise, and loving pals. If they had said, "You're nuts," or, "That's not from God, dude," then I would've dropped those ideas. But they didn't. They thought about them, considered them, prayed about them, and then gave me the thumbs-up.

Those were just some of the seeds God wanted to plant just in me.

TUNING IN TO CHANNEL 41

When I was a ten, I had a portable, black-and-white TV in my bedroom. I loved that thing because it let me watch old reruns of *The Twilight Zone* on Friday nights at 10:30 on Kansas City's most popular UHF channel: 41.

Every Friday evening, after my folks had gone to sleep, I'd turn on that little TV, wait for it to "warm up," then I'd work the two metal sticks jutting out of the top of the TV.

Those two antennae were designed to receive ultra high frequency radio waves bouncing around the atmosphere.

If those antennae weren't up, all I could watch was dancing static.

With the antennae up, I could watch *The Twilight Zone*.

Only by living with our spiritual antennae up will we pick up what words God is trying to say to us.

That means actually reading the Bible. My Bible has never suddenly popped open on its own, shooting a verse out of it that smacks me across the face. God speaks to me through the Bible pretty much only when I'm reading the Bible or remembering what I read in the Bible.

It also means exposing yourself to good teachers and books, sermons, lectures, and writings that seem to point to God and point to truth.

It means spending time with friends who are good for you—who know you, love you, and are wise Jesus followers. It means not isolating yourself but rather opening yourself up to them. It means asking their opinion on things and telling them you're willing to hear out anything they may have to say.

It means praying. Trust me: I'm not a great pray-er, but I've learned that by sitting quietly and talking to God, I'm much more prone to get a sense of what He might be saying.

It means noting any time something you run across—something a friend says, an event that happens to you, something you read in the Bible, a song you hear—seems to reaffirm the word you think God's speaking to you. It means you take it as God going, "Yes. Yes. Yes. You're on the right track."

Really, living with your antennae up is about living a life that's a true friendship with God. It's realizing He's always near, and He seems happy to tell you what His word is for you.

I encourage you to open yourself up to—and hold onto—whatever word God might have for you. It could come in the form of a big giant truth like:

God really loves you.

You are valuable.

All humans are made in God's image.

Patient endurance is a necessary trait.

The only real security is found in God.

Pursuing wisdom is a good way to live.

Or it may come in the form of direction or insights specific to you:

Break up with that guy/girl. That relationship is bringing you both down.

Call your parents.

Learn more about Africa and what God is doing there.

Read the Book of Joshua.

Worship God when you suffer.

Use your time wisely.

Don't do any work on Sundays.

Give that homeless guy your leftovers and tell him that, even though you don't know him, you love him.

Be willing to receive the word of God for you . . . like a field willingly receives a seed.

Three Questions

What's one word of God you think God has communicated to you through the Bible?

What's one word of God you think God has communicated to you through a friend?

What word of God do you think God may be trying to communicate to you today?

Chapter 6
The Sowing

Other seed fell on good soil, where it produced a crop—a hundred, sixty or thirty times what was sown.

—Matthew 13:8

It's taken weeks of work, but the field is fit for seed. The Farmer has cast a vision for the crops he'd like to grow in the field. He's cleared out the large rocks, stumps, and major weed patches. He's created a plan for what seed should be planted where. One Friday He even poured out poultry manure all across the field. The smell wasn't appealing, but the Farmer knows manure acts like a soil steroid—whatever's planted in it grows up stronger, larger, and more fruitful. He then plowed the field, creating long, parallel furrows up and down the acres.

The earth looks beautiful to him. The soil almost looks fluffy—tilled and turned until it seems to froth up miniature bunkers, lining the furrows. Line upon line upon line. The land is flecked with spots of white—minerals left over from where the boulders once sat, healthy residue that will feed the plants, helping them grow.

The field is ready for the seed.

There are a dozen, high-priced seed-spewing machines that would make the Farmer's seed-sowing work fast and easy. But he's not about fast and easy. He's about the experience and about appreciating the connection he makes with the field through sowing the seed. So though it will take much longer, the Farmer straps a heavy bag of seed over his shoulder and heads out.

He digs his hand into the bag, bringing out a fistful of wheat seed. As he walks along the furrows of the back ten acres, he gently drops them into the furrows, creating long dotted lines of wheat seed. They barely make a sound as the seeds touch the earth.

He then pats the soil—softly, kindly, delicately—over the seeds, as though he's putting them to bed. He does this, line after line, furrow after furrow, under the blank gaze of a slightly cross-eyed scarecrow.

The Farmer drops the corn kernels one at a time into the tiny brown ditches. Each one looks like a single shining star set against a dark night sky.

He flings the cottonseed wide and far, watching it gently glide down to the ground.

It takes longer for him to empty his bag of apple seeds because there's something about those seeds that makes the Farmer pause with each handful and just admire them. He can't help but laugh at the natural law he's working from. It sounds so ridiculous! Put a tiny seed in the ground—taken from a piece of fruit—then wait. Eventually, a mighty, sturdy, burly, brown-barked, green-leafed tree with swinging branches and a trunk as thick as a Roman column will grow up. And from that tree, apples will fall. He laughs again. It all seems foolish and strange, and yet he knows it's the truth.

He needs his gloves to handle the thorny, prickly rose bushes. Keeping his face held away from the barbs, he places them in their designated holes. With a shovel, he *tosses mineral-laden soil around the bases of the bushes. Again, they're quite unremarkable-looking bushes. But they'll become something much more. (They remind the Farmer of a movie he once saw where a homely, put-upon slave girl is revealed to be a beautiful princess in disguise by film's end.)*

When the planting is done, the Farmer allows himself a moment's satisfaction. The seed has been placed within the field. It's ready to grow and change into something more.

THE FATE OF THE SEED

Let's go back to when Jesus told the group of people the metaphor of the farmer and the seed.

> A farmer went out to sow his seed. As he was scattering the seed, some fell along the path, and the birds came and ate it up. Some fell on rocky places, where it did not have much soil. It sprang up quickly, because the soil was shallow. But when the sun came up, the plants were scorched, and they withered because they had no root. Other seed fell among thorns, which grew up and choked the plants. Still other seed fell on good soil, where it produced a crop—a hundred, sixty or thirty times what was sown.
>
> —Matthew 13:3–8

Jesus categorized the fate of the seed in four ways:

1. Path: Birds ate it. Bad news.
2. Rocky places: The seed grew fast, but the sun baked it. Bad news.
3. Thorns: The seed got choked out. Bad news.
4. Good soil: Lots of crops. Good news.

Jesus' pals came up to Him after He was done talking with the people and basically said, "Now, Jesus, of course *we* get what you were trying to say with that farming metaphor, but those other people, they probably had *no* idea what you were saying. Ha, ha. Those guys . . . Anyhow, maybe you should shed some light on what all that meant? Not for us, of course. Ha, ha. No. But for those commoners."

After presumably rolling His eyes so hard they launched into space, Jesus let His friends in on what the elements of the metaphor represent.

The seed is the word of God.

Seed falling on the path is when a person hears a word from God, but Satan comes and takes away the word (v. 19).

Seed falling in the rocky places is when a person hears a word from God, receives it "with joy," but when "trouble or persecution" comes, the seed stops growing (vv. 20–21).

Seed falling among thorns is when "the worries of this life and the deceitfulness of wealth" and desires for other things choke the word, making it "unfruitful" (v. 22).

And, finally, seed falling on good soil is when someone hears the word, accepts it, and it produces a crop—"a hundred, sixty or thirty times what was sown" (v. 23).

Jesus was saying in categorical terms, three bad things can happen to something I want to communicate to you and one good thing.

That's a lot going against the little seed, isn't it?

Let's not think about something so hopeless and depressing. Instead let's think of something happy: like Snicker bars chopped up inside strawberry ice cream. Seriously, this is a wonderful concoction, and if you're turning your nose up at it right now it's only because you haven't ever actually tried it.

Okay, that's enough distraction from tough stuff. We need to think about this some more because there's a lot at stake.

If that seed dies (falling on the path, with the rocks, among the thorns), it's not going to bring about the crop of good things God wants to grow in us.

So let's consider each of these scenarios a little more to see how they play out in in real life.

LIES

> As soon as they hear it, Satan comes and takes away the word that was sown in them.
>
> —Mark 4:15

A couple of years back, I heard Mae Mae playing with stuff under the sink in her bathroom. I'm pretty sure old thermometers and cleaning bleach aren't the best toys for a three-year-old, so I went to investigate. When I found her, standing there before the open cabinet, our conversation went like this:

Me: *Mae Mae, were you playing with the stuff under your sink?*

Mae Mae: *Yes. But I was just—*

Me: *Okay. No more playing with the stuff under your sink. Okay?*

Mae Mae doesn't say anything. She just stares at all that fun stuff under the sink. She turns back to me and notices I don't seem to be leaving her room.

Mae Mae: *Daddy, would you go downstairs now?*

Me: *Why?*

Mae Mae: *Would you just go downstairs, please?*

Clearly, Mae Mae is bad at lying. I can see through what she's saying to her plan: Daddy goes downstairs, and I go back to playing with bottles of expired Tylenol.

One day, though, she's going to get good at lying. And when she does, our house will probably go a little crazy. Why? Because lies mess everything up.

When we're lied to—by daughters, friends, coworkers, bosses, politicians, anyone in authority, anyone we're in charge of—it's hard to keep our bearings. It's like having a busted compass. It's like trying to make your way through the *Poseidon*. (*The Poseidon Adventure* is an old movie about an overturned cruise ship and Gene Hackman saving the day in an awesome white turtleneck).

All throughout Jesus' life, He talked about Satan—the devil. The concept of the devil probably sounds weird to our modern ears because we feel a little too sophisticated to believe in a goateed dude in a red suit with a bifurcated tail. But Bugs Bunny cartoons are probably not the most reliable means of getting a clear understanding of spiritual beings.

Jesus defines Satan as "the deceiver"—a grand liar. He lies because he's bent on keeping anything good from coming to anyone on earth. Jesus says Satan lives to "steal and kill and destroy" (John 10:10). This hateful being does this primarily through lies.

These lies are designed to fly against the words of God—God's truth—spoken to us, because the words of God bring goodness and life to us.

And Satan hates us having life.

So Satan takes God's truth and communicates the opposite to us. Or he tries to convince us the truth God has given us isn't really true and isn't really from God.

Growing up, my parents took me to church at least twice a week. We'd go on Sunday mornings where I'd attend Sunday school (imagine a room full of kids singing "Jesus Loves Me" with absolutely no regard for key or tune, then listening to someone tell the story of Zacchaeus with little figures glued to popsicle sticks, and then doing a craft that, I'm sure, my parents morally struggled with throwing away immediately) and then the Big Church service. We'd usually come back Sunday nights for another Big Church-type service. Often, we'd go to the Wednesday night prayer meeting. And sometimes my parents had a choir rehearsal in there somewhere.

Growing up, I heard a lot about God and Jesus.

But it wasn't until high school that the idea of forgiveness really started to kick in. I'd always heard about the Cross and Jesus' sacrifice, but nothing in my heart connected how, through that act, God forgave me of what I'd done wrong.

When that happened, it was a really cool thing. The more I became aware of my sin—everything I'd done wrong, any time I'd disagreed with God and what He knew was best for me and went in a different direction anyway—the more I realized how amazing God's forgiveness was.

I'd lie in bed at night thinking of things I'd done in the past. Like hitting my sister when I was a kid, that time I cheated on a math test in first grade, talking back to my mom. Then I came to the stark realization of how great it was that God didn't hold that stuff against me.

Forgiveness was good. I realized it was God's word to all of the world, but I really felt like it was important for me. That seed was meant to grow a great crop—a crop that had to do with security in His love and grace and, by extension, a willingness to forgive others.

Good seed, great crop.

That lying, conniving, deceiving Satan, though, didn't like any of that. He knew I was on the verge of living a much better life because I was about to be less concerned with trying to work to do good things in an effort to offset the balance of the bad things I'd done and more concerned about resting in God's forgiveness for everything in my past.

Satan hates life. He hates me having life. Heck, he hates me enjoying life.

(And living in forgiveness really does lead to enjoyment of life.)

So what did the liar start doing? He started to lie to me.

But he's crafty. Rarely does he go in the exact opposite of what God has said. If God were to say something like, "I want you to know that $1,297 + 42 = 1,339$," Satan doesn't really go, "No. It equals 2,687,310." He's more subtle than that. He's more like, "Well, is that 1,297 even the right number to start with? Probably not. Who even likes that number? If you asked someone what their favorite number was, would anyone on earth say, 'Uh, probably 1,297'? No! Never! So why are we even bothering with this? This is irrelevant. We shouldn't be thinking about all of this."

He lies.

Satan didn't start to impress upon me that God hadn't really forgiven me of things in my past. That would've been too blatant, and, more than likely, the stark contrast between that and what God had communicated clearly through the Bible and teachers and my family would've made me go, "Duh. That's a lie. Next."

Instead he started to communicate this to me:

"Oh, yeah. God forgives you for all that stuff in your past. I mean, that's clear in the Bible. Good job believing all that. So I guess it's your job now to not sin, right? I mean, God's forgiven your past—thank goodness, right?!—but from here on out it's up to you. Jesus dying on the Cross only covered your past."

I genuinely started thinking being "saved" just meant having my past forgiven. From there on out, it was up to me to . . . always . . . do . . . what's right.

That translated into me working hard to be perfect. As you may expect, that did not go well.

When I ended up sinning, I found myself steeped in guilt and shame. "God forgave my past. But this new sin isn't covered. *Ugh.*"

And that made me go nuts. It made me try to be better and better and better.

Eventually I started to lose life—the very life God wanted to give me.

God had given me a word: "You're forgiven!" He dropped a seed on my field in hopes of growing something wonderful. Instead Satan lied to me. And, in no time, a bird had gobbled up the seed and taken it away.

No seed, no crop.

What had gone wrong? A few things. At the time I didn't have many people I felt comfortable enough around to talk about big spiritual things. So I suffered in silence, not questioning this lie. I also don't think I knew how to vet this idea through the Bible. I also think some of the teachers I was listening to at the time were more about moral living than God's constant stream of forgiveness. I didn't have the tools necessary to combat the devil's lies.

It's a longer story, but when God showed me that Satan was lying to me and that God's forgiveness via the Cross didn't just cover my past but also any sin I would every commit beyond that, I had the biggest, most freeing and radical breakthrough of my entire life. I genuinely see my life as being broken into two parts: the years before I realized this truth and the time since. It was the moment I truly experienced grace and God's love, and I've never been the same. A good crop ended up coming from the seed after all.

I learned through that whole experience—and many others since—that if I ever feel like God's communicated something to me but then I start to get the idea that what I thought He'd communicated to me isn't totally true, I need to check in with the Bible. And listen to teaching about it. And hit up my Jesus-following friends for advice. And pray. If I don't do those things, I'll fall for anything.

I deal with speaker coaching clients who have trouble becoming better speakers because they're believing lies. I see it all the time. I worked with an incredibly powerful, high-in-the-ranks, regularly-interviewed-by-*Fortune*-magazine woman who should've been one of the most confident people in the business world. She wasn't. This bright, insightful, effective leader felt like a fraud when she took the stage. When I asked her about it, she choked up and said she was an imposter. We talked about that for a while and eventually worked through that lie when it came to her presenting. Left unchecked, that untruth would've kept her from truly becoming the leader she was meant to be.

When God tells you something, Satan hates it because it will bring you life. And he hates you experiencing life. So he will use manipulation to distort truth. He will lie to you. He will. I promise. As Paul says, be aware of the devil's schemes, and be ready to respond to fight those lies. Make sure that seed bounces off the path and onto good soil.

RESISTANCE

> Others, like seed sown on rocky places, hear the word and
> at once receive it with joy. But since they have no root, they
> last only a short time. When trouble or persecution comes
> because of the word, they quickly fall away.
>
> —Mark 4:16–17

I read a lot of creativity books. Usually these books center on getting in touch with your inner creator, tapping into your passions, or meditating your way to the world's best mystery novel.

But the best creativity book I've ever read looks at the act of creativity in a much more blue-collar, practical, get-it-done way.

In *The War of Art,* Steven Pressfield tells creative people to stop looking at creating as a wildly mysterious process that requires navel-gazing, a yoga mat, and the patience necessary to wait on an unseen muse who drops down dollops of inspiration. That's what amateurs do. Instead, creatives should work like pros. To work like a pro means we look at creative projects in the same way a plumber looks at his work. A plumber doesn't wake up in the morning and think, "I'll unclog Ms. Atkins's kitchen sink just as soon as I'm really feeling it." No! A plumber just does the work! According to Pressfield, creatives should have the same attitude and just do the work.

He adds, though, that once you set about to do the work, you're going to run into something that stands up to you, doing its best to keep you from completing your creative endeavor.

He calls it resistance.

If you consider yourself a creative type, see if this timeline doesn't sound familiar. And if you don't consider yourself a creative, see if this applies to a project around the house or at work.

You begin with an idea. "I'm going to write a novel about a French chef continuing to cook at his Parisian restaurant during German occupation in World War II." Or, "I'm going to paint a picture of the street I grew up on as a child." Or, "I'm going to draft a reorganization chart for my department to improve efficiency and communication flow." Or, "That hall closet? The one that's so overflowing a bowling ball drops on my head every time I open the door, like in a cartoon? I'm cleaning that thing out."

Next, the passion for this idea really hits you. "I love France! And World War II! And food! This will be fun writing this book!" Or, "I miss my old house so painting a picture will bring it back to life!" Or, "My department needs this re-org!" Or, "I don't like bowling balls falling on my head! Yeah!"

This passion fires you up. It's what gets you to sit down to write . . . or paint . . . or create a new organization flow chart . . . or start to pull stuff from the hall closet.

At first.

But that passion only gets you so far.

It gets you through three pages of the novel. (Or Act One of your script.) Or a half-formed pencil sketch on a canvas. Or three people imagined in different positions on the org chart. Or the winter jackets pulled out of the closet.

Then resistance hits.

Resistance reminds you what a massive task you've decided to undertake.

"Um, you know you're three pages into your novel, and you're already out of character names (you've used "Jacques" for two different people already). Writing a book is hard work, and you have about four hundred more pages to write."

"You know you don't know how to work with perspective, right? Like, yeah, you sketched the right angles on your house, but you have no idea how to line those up with the other houses and the street and the horizon line. You have a long way to go and a lot to learn. Also, that bush out front looks crooked."

"Jamie can go in that position. Yes. But, everyone else is going to be angry she got that position—especially Hank. You have to move everyone around to make the org better, but you can't make anyone quit. This is like an organizational Rubik's Cube—and you've always hated Rubik's Cubes."

"Great. The scarves are organized. Now all you have left is the dozen empty duffel bags, fourteen parkas, a bunch of old baseball hats, that pile of crumbled granola bar bits in the corner, a bunch of baseballs and golf balls, a box of photos, and nine binders filled with old college papers. And that's just the left side. Good luck, bud."

Resistance reminds you how Herculean the task before you is. It tells you that you don't have the tools necessary to complete it. It accuses you of delusions of grandeur for thinking you could possibly do this. Then resistance does one other tricky thing—

—it reminds you of things you could be doing that are much, much easier.

"Hey, instead of writing this book, why don't we go and research World War II? Maybe by watching *The Dirty Dozen* for the eighty-seventh time. Or maybe all of *Band of Brothers*. Didn't Tom Hanks produce that? Maybe we should watch *Sleepless in Seattle* too because he's in that and that's a great movie."

"Painting this street is too hard. Let's just search on Facebook for the name of that weird girl who lived down the street from me—the one who used to pour her chocolate milk down the cracks of the sidewalk thinking she was drowning trolls, saying, 'Take that, *trolls!*' Besides, I bet a lot of interesting updates have happened on Facebook since I checked it ten minutes ago."

"My company is fine. I don't get paid enough to do extra-credit work like this. Also no one's going to like what I propose. I'll just go back to performing the simplest part of my job: sitting in this chair, looking busy."

"The closet? No way. Let's take a nap! Yay! *Zzzzz.*"

And, in no time, your idea—and the passion behind it—has fizzled. The original idea sits up on a mental shelf, next to all of the other ideas you've had that didn't go anywhere.

Jesus says there will be resistance when we receive a word from Him.

He says that in many instances, people will receive what God has to say with joy. They hear something from God and go, "This is great! I love this! This is going to help my life! What a great seed! Thanks, God!"

Jesus isn't against us being excited about what He's communicated to us. He just knows that initial excitement doesn't matter nearly as much as what we do with the seeds a week, two weeks, three months, a year later.

He says how we respond to resistance—trouble and persecution—is the true indicator of how we feel about the truth He's given us.

Trouble and persecution are two more tools that hang right next to lies on Satan's evil tool belt. Whereas lies seem to come from inside ourselves as Satan whispers to us, trouble and persecution come from outside of us.

Trouble and persecution are what happen when the going gets tough. When walking out what God has talked to us about gets hard to do.

Let's say God has a word for a guy named Tim. Through a verse in the Bible, something he hears a teacher say, and something a buddy tells him, Tim realizes God wants him to be a better, more present husband to his wife Kate.

When Tim realizes what God's saying, he knows it's good for him. He realizes his wife has become cynical and kind of cold primarily because Tim has been self-centered and checked-out. Instead of making him feel like a bad person, it actually excites him because he realizes his marriage can improve.

Tim is full of joy. "I'm gonna do this! I'm gonna love and serve my wife! I'll put my phone down when she's talking to me! Tonight—yes, tonight!—I'll come home and ask her what *she* wants to do for dinner! And I'm not going to tell her where I want to go—I'm going to ask *her*!"

"Best insight ever," Tim says to himself. Then Tim gets home that evening:

Tim: *Kate! Dinner tonight! Where do you want to go?*

Kate: *I don't really care.*

Tim: *I'm letting you decide, honey!*

Kate: *Really, I don't care. Where do you want to—*

Tim: *No! Kate! I'm letting you decide! Isn't this great?!*

Kate: *But I really don't have anywhere in mind. Do you have any ideas?*

Tim: *Ha, ha! Kate, really, this is your decision!*

Kate: *I could just stay at home and eat here. Save some money.*

Tim: *Wait, what? No. We're going out to eat. Now, where do you want to—*

Kate: *Give me some suggestions.*

Tim: *I don't have any suggestions! I'm letting you decide!*

Kate: *But, I don't really care—*

Tim: *You don't care?! Seriously?! You don't care?!*

Kate: *Yes! That's what I said!*

Tim: *This is unbelievable.*

Kate: *What's unbelievable?!*

Tim: *You! This! I'm just trying to let you choose!*

Kate: *But I don't care—*

Tim: *Fine. We're going to Chili's.*

Kate: *Well . . . not there, maybe.*

Tim then stomps off to the garage where, for the next three hours, he tries to change the oil in his car even though he's never done that before and has no idea how to do it and doesn't even have any oil to put into the car but he just needs to be alone until bedtime, and what's so wrong with Chili's, and no wonder Tim's selfish and checked-out because Kate won't even tell him what she wants and why bother?

Tim got a word from God.

Tim was excited about the word from God.

Then it got hard to implement that word from God.

So Tim gave up on the endeavor altogether.

Resistance stands in the space between the initial joy a word from God brings us and actively putting it into practice over a long period of time.

Resistance always comes when God speaks a word. Always.

And when it does, it's easy for us to just go back to how we were before the word was spoken. We avoid how hard it is to live out the word and go toward our default, easy way of living.

We drift toward what feels good and easy in the short term, not for what's more challenging—but ultimately beneficial—in the long term.

Young athletes give up when their natural ability only gets them so far and they get to a point where they genuinely have to push themselves to get better.

Artists and writers create according to their instincts, but when it comes time to do the challenging work of improving their craft, they give in to resistance and just create the way they always have.

It's hard for my clients to improve as speakers because it's not necessarily a comfortable process. That discomfort makes a lot of them do whatever it takes to skip our sessions and avoid the work of development.

If a seed's going to grow, it needs deep roots, not just initial passion. Deep roots come from pushing through resistance— trouble and persecution—until something good eventually grows up.

A bit of poet Edgar Guest's "See It Through" gives us a bit of encouragement here:

> Even hope may seem but futile,
>   When with troubles you're beset,
> But remember you are facing
>   Just what other men have met.
> You may fail, but fall still fighting;
>   Don't give up, whate'er you do;
> Eyes front, head high to the finish.
>   See it through!

DISTRACTIONS

> Still others, like seed sown among thorns, hear the word;
> but the worries of this life, the deceitfulness of wealth and
> the desires for other things come in and choke the word,
> making it unfruitful.
>
> —Mark 4:18–19

Let's go back to the hall closet. That thing is a mess. You have multiple lumps on your head because of the falling bowling ball. You think there's a vacuum hidden somewhere in the back of the closet, but you can't get to it without a headlamp and a machete.

It's important for you to clean out that closet. And it's going to take some work. Not just five minutes of reorganization but *hours*. And those hours will probably have to be spread out over an entire Saturday.

At first, something in you tells you that you don't really need— or even want—a clean closet. "Yes, it's a mess, but I know where everything is!" You also get the classic line: "What, are you a neat freak?" "This is not worth my time."

But you fight through those lies. You remind yourself of the good that will come from actually doing this thing, getting that closet cleaned out.

You even push through resistance. You don't give up after ten minutes, twenty minutes, two hours on a Saturday morning, even though the task isn't easy.

Your husband . . . or wife . . . or roommate . . . or kid . . . or dog . . . even makes fun of you. "I guess you have to get that done today, huh? Good luck! Ha ha!" (Your dog is way too sassy, by the way.)

Still, you push through. You keep going.

Then the bar you hang coats on snaps in two. The coats all fall. Still, you push through. (Thanks, duct tape.) You keep going.

You're going to get this done. You are. It's going to happen. You're going to stay at this until, finally, that bowling ball stays put and all of the coats—

—wait, is that *Ocean's Eleven* on TV?

You're pretty sure it is. You take a few steps down the hall and look into the living room. Yep. Your wife/husband/roommate/child/dog has turned on the TV, and there's George Clooney trying to convince Brad Pitt they should put a team together and knock over a casino.

Oh, man. This is a good movie. You know it's a good movie because you've seen it roughly 147 times.

So you sit on the couch. Just for a moment.

Then it's the end of the movie. No, not the end of *Ocean's Eleven*. It's the end of *Ocean's Thirteen*. You've just sat on the couch and watched all of *Ocean's Eleven* and *Ocean's Twelve* (the bad one) and *Ocean's Thirteen*.

You just sat through cable TV's *Ocean's* marathon.

What . . . just . . . happened?

You had a goal, you had a plan, you pushed through resistance, and then . . .

. . . you got distracted.

Oops.

And now you're sad.

Jesus didn't really talk much about closets (except for praying inside them), but He talked plenty about distractions.

In this part of the seed metaphor, Jesus predicts that many people will receive a word from God, but it won't become an actual crop because things like comfort, worries, and the pursuit of money will distract the people from harvesting.

This happens all of the time.

About a year ago, my wife and I realized we were both really struggling with jealousy. I know jealousy sounds like the kind of thing only, say, thirteen-year-old middle school girls struggle with—"Dad, why does she have a new pair of Those Awesome Shoes and I don't? She gets everything she wants. I hate my life. Sad-face emoji."—but it was a real thing for us.

When friends would get a new house, we'd initially say, "Yay," but that excitement soon morphed into, "Why not us?" And when other friends got to go on a big, cool vacation, we'd be happy for them . . . then sad for us.

It wasn't pretty.

Around that time, Bob, an incredibly wise friend of mine, emailed me his notes for a talk he'd recently given. Now when Bob sends me his speaking points, I sit up and take notice. Why? Because Bob is thoroughly brilliant while also being radically inspiring. Bob's world famous (literally) for both of those qualities. When he gives talks, they're to people like the governing body of the Philippines or Oxford grad students or the king of Bhutan.

The notes Bob sent were from a talk he gave on gratitude. In the talk, Bob cited case studies and data, which showed that the more grateful people were, the happier they were. Psychologists had discovered that by simply expressing gratitude on a daily basis (whether to God or some cloud drifting by in the sky), people could actually lead happier and more satisfied lives.

That grabbed me. Especially in the light of the Fog of Moping that had descended on House Davenport.

So my wife and I talked, and we decided to practice gratefulness on a regular basis. We committed to doing one thing a day to communicate to God we were actually grateful for something He'd given us that day.

We also knew it would be a good way to teach Mae Mae about gratefulness. (Bomber, at the time, was too young. Her idea of showing gratitude was not vomiting on us.)

We placed a big, round glass vase on our kitchen table. My wife picked up a bag of glass rocks (that's the best way I can describe them) and scattered them around the edge of the vase. We added a Sharpie to the set-up.

Every night at dinner, we would go around and each say one thing we were thankful for, and I would use the Sharpie to write it on a rock. Then we'd put our rocks in the vase. We had a pretty big variety of things written on rocks: a car that worked, my job, Bomber not vomiting on us that day, "Baby" (Mae Mae's cleverly named baby doll), enchiladas, friends, sunshine, candy bar-infused ice cream. Lots of great stuff.

We really got a kick out of doing it. And, honestly, it seemed to help lighten our mood and get us focused on God and what He had given us—rather than what He hadn't.

Looking back, it seems that God communicated His word to us Davs: "Be grateful! It'll help!" and we acted on it. We did what He'd instructed us to do, and we started growing up a nice little crop of contentedness and focus on God.

After going strong for nine months or so, our gratefulness petered out though. Why? Because we got distracted. My wife and I focused on other things during the times when we had been focusing on gratitude. The girls would go down, and she and I would eat dinner together, but we'd do it while mindlessly wandering through the Netflix forest. And that little ritual of being grateful and jotting it down just . . . kind of . . . went away.

Not long after, we started to go back to grousing about our situation. Discontentedness started rearing its ugly head more and more. We got mopey again. We said, "Why not us?" more.

It's easy to get distracted. It's easy to focus on other things. It's easy to (as they say in baseball) take your eye off the ball. It's really, really easy.

It took more time than I'd care to admit but, eventually, we realized we'd slipped back into The Funk. So we reinstated the thankfulness ritual. Since it was autumn, my wife cut cute little leaf shapes from construction paper, and we wrote out what we were each thankful for on a paper leaf and taped it to the mantel. Soon, our mantel was covered in these leaves, and we had a reminder—right there in our living room—that God was consistently good to us, and it's foolish to sit around thinking He's not.

We had to overcome distraction, though, to get back to that state of mind. Not easy, but it was worth it.

A friend of mine ended up letting go of a beautiful seed God had planted in Him—a seed meant to help him walk more and more in freedom, realizing He was a loved son—because he didn't think he had time to feed that seed. His kids were in an expensive school and his family had gotten used to a certain standard of living, so he gave more and more of his time over to pursuing his career . . . and less and less to sitting with God and letting himself be loved by his Good Father.

Only recently has the cost of being distracted from that word brought my buddy back around to it. I know he regrets letting distraction win temporarily, but now he's focused more on that word, he's more doggedly determined to stick with it than ever before.

Again, Satan uses distractions to shift our focus from the things God wants to communicate to us that will bring us life. And we're distracted all too easily.

When my pal's son was three years old, he was on a soccer team. That sounded really young for organized sports to me, so I asked him how the games went. He shrugged and said, "Oh, they're fine. Until someone flies a kite nearby. Then the whole game stops."

That's us—even as adults. We know what we're meant to be doing, but then a kite flies by—something distracting, something that takes our mind off things, pursuing pleasure, keeping up with the Joneses, chasing money—and we let ourselves get pulled away from the good thing God wants us focused on.

If we let ourselves get distracted for long enough, the memory of what God originally spoke to us may . . . slowly . . . fade away.

FROM BANDAGED TO GRABBY

Lies, resistance, and distractions. Different means with the same result: stunted growth.

God wants us to get from Point A to Point B, and then there are all these things that show up to stop us. And if lies, resistance, and distractions have their way, we end up right back where we started. We begin at Point A . . . and we end at Point A.

We get stuck in a cycle.

What's worse is that the more often we try to move from Point A to get to Point B, but end up back at Point A, the less confident we are to keep trying. Something in our minds says, "I can't change. Change isn't possible. Why keep trying?

I shouldn't keep trying," and we block our ears and stop listening for anything God could be trying to communicate because, after all, what's the use?

There's a great old poem by Rudyard Kipling called "The Gods of the Copybook Headings." He has a great phrase for getting stuck in cycles, doing the same things over and over again—especially destructive things: "The burnt Fool's bandaged finger goes wobbling back to the Fire."

We don't want to be like that fool who's burned his hand . . . and keeps burning it. Never really learning or moving on.

The only way to break the cycle is to give seed a good place to land.

So what are the defining characteristics of good soil?

I like Luke's version of the end of Jesus' seed metaphor explanation a lot: "But the seed on good soil stands for those with a noble and good heart, who hear the word, retain it, and by persevering produce a crop" (Luke 8:15).

Jesus says that good soil is . . . grabby.

Grabby. Weird word, sure. But I think it's accurate.

When my sister gave birth to her first kid Jonah, my mom became a grandma for the first time. One of the best parts of becoming a grandparent is choosing your grandparent name. My mom chose "Gabby." This is a pretty great grandma name and apropos for my mom because my mom can, as they say, "talk a chicken off the bone." (Another great similar-meaning phrase: "She talks nineteen to the dozen.")

It didn't take long though for my sister and I to jokingly switch Mom's grandma name from "Gabby" to "Grabby." We did this because it didn't matter who was holding baby Jonah, my Mom was going to find a way to grab that kid back and hold him herself.

She loved being a grandma. And she loved Jonah. She just wanted him in her arms. She wanted to coo at him, calm him, help him fall asleep, and admire him.

Gabby was grabby.

And it was a beautiful thing.

"Grabby" describes someone who so values something that they want to hold onto it with all of their might. They love the thing so they grasp it. They don't want to let go without a fight.

I'm grabby about my ice cream. When I dish up a big bowl of strawberry ice cream with Snickers chunks in it for myself and then I ask my wife if she wants me to serve her up any, and she says no . . . but then *fifteen seconds later* she's asking for bite out of my bowl, I get grabby.

Mae Mae is very, very grabby with her Baby. Bomber tries to get it from her, but Mae Mae holds it even tighter.

Bomber is grabby with her tiny, white blankie. Good luck getting that thing out of her little hands when she doesn't want you to have it. Those hands become hydraulic vices.

My wife is grabby about her times to go on a run. It's important to her, and she gets frustrated and a little bit grumpy if she misses those run times two days in a row.

We get grabby when something really matters to us. When we realize its importance to us and our lives (or, in my case, my stomach). Grabby is a natural response to things we genuinely want. I didn't have to teach Bomber to be grabby about her blankie.

Matthew quotes Jesus as saying good soil is about people who hear and understand. When a concept was important for me to learn in school, I did what I could to understand it. And when I understood it, it became mine. When you work to understand something, you prove you're grabby about it.

Mark quotes Jesus as saying good soil is about people who hear and accept (4:20). Acceptance is a form of grabbiness. When someone buys me a gift, I have a choice: I can either accept the gift or reject the gift. There are number of reasons to reject a gift ("It's too expensive!" "I didn't get you anything!" "I really don't like this!") but there's one main reason to accept a gift: "I really want this."

Luke quotes Jesus as saying good soil is about people who hear, retain, and persevere (Luke 8:15). That word *retain* is a great one. It indicates holding onto something for more than just a moment. Anyone can hand me something—like a guy passing out flyers on the street. I may let him stick one in my hand, but I'm not retaining that thing. I'm putting it into a trash can as soon as I can. When I was in college, teachers talked about retaining information all the time. They didn't want us to just learn a concept so we could pass the exam. They wanted us to retain the knowledge for years to come so we could apply it throughout our careers and lives. I retained anything they taught me—I got mentally grabby with it—if I was convinced it was going to be good for me.

I think the first, best step to filling our field with good soil is to receive the seed well. It's important for us to be grabby for it—wanting and valuing it. The bad soil scenarios all revolve around the field/person not truly "holding dear" the seed. Even in the situation when someone receives it with joy, it's clear the person doesn't truly, deeply value the seed more than other things in this world because it gets relegated to a lower priority and then gobbled up.

How important is growth to us? Do we look at us growing as humans—growing into the image of Jesus—and growing things inside of us to help us live better lives and to help others as truly, vitally important? Or is that kind of growth a passing fancy, a whim, something that seems like a good idea—until it gets difficult?

Many times in my life I've seen growth as an option, not a necessity. Like it was an elective class, not a part of my major. And, to be honest, when that was the case, no growth ever happened. I didn't value the seed enough, so I didn't do what it took to give it a good place to land, a place where it could turn into fruit.

Do we really believe growth is a necessity? Do we really value and appreciate the words God gives us?

A field with good soil receives the seed with deep appreciation, highly valuing the seed and what it will become.

It realizes that forces will come along to destroy the seed.

And a field with good soil takes the steps necessary to protect that seed.

Why?

So it can grow into something wonderful.

Three Questions

When is a time in your life when a word of God didn't produce a crop because of lies, resistance, or distraction?

Where are you facing lies, resistance, or distraction today?

What do you think God wants you to be "grabby" about?

Chapter 7
The Growing

Who dares despise the day of small things?

—Zechariah 4:10

With the seed in the ground, the Farmer turns his attention to ensuring it grows. This part of the work isn't over in a day, or even a week. It's the work of months. And often years. But he's up for it.

One of his consistent chores is making sure each seed—and, eventually, each seedling, bush, plant, and tree—gets the water it needs. Sometimes this means dragging a hose out to specific acres, soaking them in the wet, life-giving goodness. Other days it means watching the skies, keeping a hopeful eye open for pregnant gray rainclouds, scooting across the horizon. Sometimes it means he's covering plants to protect them from frozen water like hail and frost. Water levels are constantly on his mind.

He also trains an eye on the sun while noting the level of mercury in the thermometer hanging just outside the barn door. On days when the sun is just a bit too brutal, he drags a light tarp across the field, draping it over tender shoots. On days when the sun is just right—not too close, not too far away—he gives himself a few minutes to watch and marvel at the mysterious engine of photosynthesis as the sunlight is turned into energy and food.

Crows seem to delight in swooping down and grabbing up every seed, seedling, or sign of bud they can find. The Farmer hammers out and stuffs a dozen more scarecrows and dots the acreage with them. Most of the time they work as intended. When they don't, the Farmer chases the angry black birds away with a shovel and a guttural shout.

He's a little more kind to the deer who wander onto the land looking for a nibble from a rose bush or a few carrot stems. For them, he scatters old corncobs with stale niblets still stuck on them out behind the barn. The deer eat them and are satisfied—keeping them from the fresh young crops growing up.

On most days the Farmer's jobs are small—single tasks that take no longer than a few hours. On other days, he has to do bigger tasks requiring more time. Like building a shelter for the lettuce patch to protect it during the dog days of summer. Or stabilizing the young, top-heavy apple trees with two-by-fours and wire to keep them from toppling over on windy days. Or running chicken wire fencing around the potatoes to keep rabbits at bay.

He never turns a blind eye to weeds. Any uninvited vegetation, growing where it shouldn't, gets pulled—no questions asked.

Most days he's in the field, doing the work.

Other days he's on the porch, looking out at the field, resting and letting nature take its course. He knows that even when he's not doing something, growth is happening.

Every day, though, he spends a few moments—just as the sun comes up and just as it's going down—daydreaming about the crops. And how he'll enjoy them. And how others will too.

*Every morning and every evening he says quietly to himself,
"It's worth it. It's all worth it."*

AN INEFFICIENT WAY TO EMPTY THE DISHWASHER

In the Farmer and the field story, the Farmer's doing work while the field just kind of seems to . . . sit there.

That's not totally inaccurate.

But it's not totally accurate either.

When it comes to growing seed into crops, God does the real work behind the scenes.

But He also invites us into the process.

As Paul said, "we are co-workers in God's service" (1 Corinthians 3:9).

He works. We work. Good things come.

Of course if He wanted to, God could snap His giant God fingers and—*BOOM!*—we'd have growth. It'd be done in an instant.

So why does He let us take part in the process? Does He need our little hands working alongside His?

Question: *What's the fastest, most efficient, best way to empty a dishwasher?*

Answer: *Have a four-year-old help you.*

Wait. No. That's the exact wrong answer. If there's an efficient way, then having a four-year-old help is the opposite of that way.

Why? Because if she picks up the heavy drinking glasses, she'll probably drop them, shattering them on the floor. And she can't reach where the plates go. And every time she picks up a fork, you have to remind her to keep the sharp end pointed down. And she's slow. Like, really slow. Slow as molasses in January, as my father says.

154

Then why would I use a four-year-old to help me empty the dishwasher?

No, seriously. I'm asking. Why? Because I'm still trying to figure that out . . .

Actually I know why I let Bomber help me: because I want to spend time doing something with her, and I love that she's learning to take a part in how our house runs. It's good for her to do a little work—just like when my dad told me to get a job when I was sixteen. Also, honestly, she loves it. She begs to help. (Remember begging your dad to let you mow the lawn when you were a kid? And how much fun it was? Until . . . it became your weekly chore? And then you hated doing it?)

It's good for Bomber to help—even though I'd get it all done a lot quicker without her.

But the primary point is not to empty the dishwasher. The primary point is to help her grow as a person and to spend buddy time with my little girl.

God wants us playing a part in our growth. He knows it's good for us to participate. And God wants buddy time with us.

He invites us into the growing good things process. He wants us taking an active part in it—not to just sit idly by while He does everything (though idleness is an important part sometimes, as we'll see).

God could've waved His giant hand and suddenly given me perseverance. But He didn't. Instead He allowed me to take part in the growth process.

Sometimes I did my part well. Sometimes I didn't. Despite all the ups and downs, though, I'm finally starting to enjoy the fruit of perseverance.

So what is our part in the process . . . and what isn't?

WHAT WAS THAT AGAIN?

Some time ago, when it became clear God wanted to grow perseverance in me, I quickly forgot it.

That's crazy, right? After a lifetime of avoiding hard work, lacking stick-to-itiveness, and dodging challenges, God seemed ready to change my patterns and bring about a perseverance crop in me. That's something I knew I needed and would be beneficial to the people around me—including my wife and my kids.

So it hardly makes any sense I would forget something as important as that.

Now I have to admit, there wasn't one day on the calendar when suddenly God revealed to me He was going to start growing perseverance on my field. There's no date circled in red on my calendar.

It was something God spoke to me over a longer period of time. Through Bible verses. And moments He highlighted in my life. And by showing me the perseverance I admired in other people.

When it finally became clear God wanted to grow perseverance in me, you'd think there would be no way it would slip my mind.

But it did. Slowly. Over time.

A few months later, I read something or heard something or saw something that reminded me of what I believed to be God's word for me: perseverance! The thought came rushing back to my brain and soul.

I didn't want to forget it again, so I . . . wrote it down.

I know that doesn't sound like a massively creative step in the process, but I've found it's actually a massively important step in the process.

I did things to remind myself of what God was doing. Reminding myself is something I've come to learn myself needs to help myself. (C'mon, myself! Be a buddy and help myself!)

Once I was reminded of what God wanted to grow in me, I took a notecard (I love 'em) and a permanent marker and wrote in big, block letters PERSEVERANCE. I set that card on my desk where I would see it every day, all throughout my workday.

This visual was helpful because it kept God's end goal right in front of me.

It also reminded me to constantly look at Scripture, teachings, interactions with friends, and prayer times through this lens. It didn't mean everything I'd learn would be about perseverance, but it at least reminded me to be on the lookout for anything about it.

For instance, one morning I was reading the Bible, and I ran across this verse: "Strengthen your feeble arms and weak knees" (Hebrews 12:12).

And I felt like it was "for me," for this season.

Whenever I was sitting at my desk and something at work felt like a difficult challenge, I'd see my PERSEVERANCE notecard, and it would remind me: challenges can be opportunities. Stick with it. Take small steps to exercise this. By moving forward—even slowly—you'll help grow perseverance in you.

It's too easy to lose track of important ideas and concepts. I remember an old pastor telling husbands that if their wives told them something they could do to make them feel loved, those husbands should write it down in a notebook. He knew that for men to act on an insight, we have to remind ourselves of it. Otherwise it gets lost.

You'd think we'd naturally just remember what's of such high importance, but I've found that even the core concepts of how much Jesus loves us and how good for us it is to trust Him can get lost in the shuffle of life.

I'm not a tattoo guy, but I think this is why some people get single words or phrases they feel are important to their lives inked up on their bodies. It's because they don't trust themselves to remember something they currently feel is very, very important.

I tell clients to write big notes to themselves about their delivery ("DON'T HIDE BEHIND THE PODIUM!," "BE LOUDER THAN NATURAL!," "THEY WANT TO HEAR WHAT YOU HAVE TO SAY!") and put them on the floor of the stage where only they can see them. If they don't, they won't remember the things we worked on, and they won't deliver the way I know they can.

We forget! We do. If you don't think so, tell me your grandma's birthday. You don't remember, do you? Yeah, we're forgetful people. (Don't beat yourself up about grandma. She's cool and forgiving.)

So remind yourself. And remind yourself. And remind yourself.

LIFE WITH PALS

The best notecard system I have is called "Kristin Davenport."

Yes, it's helpful for me to write notes and leave them on my desk, but what's more effective is telling my wife what I believe God is communicating to me and wanting to grow in me.

Of course I tell her to vet it and ensure it sounds like something God would want to do.

But it's also about her being my notecard—my reminder.

Some of my other, Jesus-loving buddies make great reminders too.

When I tell people things like, "Hey, I think God's growing perseverance in me," then I get a helping hand to identify opportunities to foster that growth, as well as someone who can ask me, from time to time, "Hey . . . how's the perseverance thing going?"

Something in me doesn't naturally want to share stuff like this. I don't know if it's my pride or if it's because I think, "This is just between me and God," but when I don't share with other people, then I miss out on their perspective, and I entrust a bit too much to my own, less-than-stellar, "When-is-grandma's-birthday-again?" memory.

My wife is a World Class Encourager, so she's naturally great at giving me the "Atta Boys" I need to stick with sticking at things. Once she found out I was allowing God to grow perseverance in me, she started identifying places in my life where little tiny perseverance sprouts were coming up through the dirt. And she'd treat them as though they were mighty oak trees. "Look at this! You've gone to the gym three times this week! This is fantastic! You're really going at this!"

Does that sound lame—getting encouragement for three measly trips to the gym? Sure. But it helps me. It keeps me going because I usually beat myself up and think things like, "Three trips to the gym? Are you serious? That's nothing. Maybe you can be proud of what you've done when you've strung together a full year of going to the gym without a break and have finished—and won—three marathons in three weeks." Kristin gives me a corrective, outside voice, that's optimistic rather than defeatist and focused on short-term wins rather than overwhelming, impossibly large, long-term goals.

When I share with other people what I feel God's growing in me, I don't only get encouragement, I also get prayer. I know my wife likes to pray about things like this for me. And my buddy Andrew likes to pray for me too. I love when Andrew prays for me because Andrew doesn't pray boring, stiff, religious prayers. He prays prayers that sound more like a son just talking to his father. And when he talks to his Father, on my behalf, I feel honored . . . and I know God responds to Andrew.

I also get great questions when I tell other people about the slowly growing crop. My pal Jeeva goes right at me when we meet up for dinner during seasons of crop growth. "So dude . . . how's the perseverance thing going? Are you being challenged? How are you doing with those challenges? Do we need one appetizer or two?" Aside from the appetizer question, those are helpful, goading, keep-Jeff-on-track questions I really need to be asked.

I also need a little needling. I need people who can poke me a bit, especially as the initial momentum of whatever it was God says to me wears off. Once the joy or passion cools, I need somebody to go, "Hey! This work is still important!" even when something inside me is going, "Yeah . . . I'm not sure that crop's such a big thing anymore." I need my buddies to go, "Really? Did God change His mind or has just the original excitement worn off?"

The poet T. S. Eliot wrote this line a long time ago: "What life have you if you have not life together?"

There is not life that is not in community,

My life comes alive more when I'm sharing it with my buddies—and my wife and my family—letting them in on the things God is doing. When I shut them out, or believe these are private matters, I miss out on life together.

I need my pals to remind me of what God is growing in me.

BE BATMAN

I don't really like comic books, and I'm not a huge comic book movie fan (even though at this point in time, roughly 86.3 percent of all movies that go to theaters revolves around a superhero). That said, I kind of like Batman.

Sure, Batman doesn't have any super powers—aside from being really rich and having a really square jaw—but that doesn't keep him from stopping the bad guys.

My favorite scenes in Batman movies are when thugs or mafia guys or jewel thieves are walking along an alley at night, thinking they've just gotten away with a crime or are on their way to committing another one. Then—out of nowhere—a dark, fast-moving shadow swoops up from behind them and knocks 'em flat to the ground. The bad guy looks up and hardly sees anything but then proceeds to have his bell rung by—what appears to be—a dude in a black rubber suit with tiny pointy ears (and a bad cold because his voice sounds scratchy).

How in the world did Batman know the bad guy would be at that place, at that time?

Batman knew because he was watching.

Batman is always watching.

Apparently sleep isn't super important to Batman because all night long, this guy's swinging around from building to building, looking for dudes with their collars turned up and crooked grins on their faces, holding pistols, fistfuls of pearl necklaces, or canvas bags marked with dollar signs.

Batman keeps the streets of Gotham safe because he keeps his eyes open. He's vigilant.

The word *vigilant* just means watchful. (The Latin root of *vigilant* is *vigilare*, which means "to stay awake.") A vigil is when you stay up all night, keeping a watch. And a vigilante is, literally, somebody who's up, scanning for danger.

Gotham Policeman: *That Batman . . . we've got to arrest him! He's a vigilante!*

Bruce Wayne: *Well, if by "vigilante" you mean "someone who stays up super, super late and watches out for bad stuff," then, yes, that courageous Batman sure is a vigilante.*

(Then Bruce yawns because he had a late night the night before.)

Gotham Policeman: *We mean he's a vigilante in the sense he breaks people's noses without giving them a trial.*

Bruce Wayne: (shrugging) *Yeah, sure. He's that too.*

In the Bible God often tells His followers to be vigilant or watchful or aware. What are they keeping an eye out for? Anything that will cause them to fall for something the enemy wants to do. Really God is saying, "Keep an eye out for Satan's schemes. Be aware of his lies."

It's important for us to keep the seed from falling into the bad, lie-filled soil by being Batman for ourselves—and allowing our pals to be our Batmen too.

We do this by constantly monitoring the messages we're allowing to sit in our heads and our hearts. We assess whether they line up with helping the seed God has planted in us—or if they actually will keep the seed from growing.

We demolish arguments and every pretension that sets itself up against the knowledge of God, and we take captive every thought to make it obedient to Christ.

—2 Corinthians 10:5

Taking every thought captive means we grab messages and compare them to truth. If they don't line up, they're tossed. Adios. Sayonara. Don't let the door catch yer heel . . .

Once perseverance started to emerge as a theme in my life—something God wanted to grow—lies started coming along, fast and furious. I started thinking things like, "I'm too old to suddenly become perseverant. That's something you learn when you're in your early twenties. If you don't learn it by then, you're doomed to just being a shiftless, lazy dude who doesn't get long-term things done." I really started thinking that: "It's too late for me. Maybe it's something I can just instill in my daughters . . ."

I also started believing lies about small efforts I was putting into the process. "Being perseverant one day? *P'shaw*. That's nothing. That doesn't even matter. Why bother with just *one day*?" Because of this lie, I got tempted to not be perseverant on a given, say, Wednesday, because, really . . . what good is one day of being perseverant?

More than a few times, I believed those lies—not because I thought, "Well, that lie sounds good," but because I thought, "That sounds like the truth." (No one actively believes a lie. Instead, they mistake a lie for the truth.)

Other times, I acted like Batman: keeping an eye out for messages like those, recognizing them as anti-seed, and punching them right in the nose.

When I'm not being Batman, I'm prone to let any old lie cross my path and pull me away from what God's intending. When I am being Batman, I keep the growth process going, ensuring the seed doesn't pop over from good soil to the rocky path.

Being vigilant for lies protects the seed and helps it grow.

LEARNING CAN BE FUN

My wife and I run a small English-as-a-second-language school out of our home. Now, before you get too impressed, understand:

When I say *small* I mean *we only have two students.*

Those two students are our daughters.

Their native language isn't French or Mandarin or Spanish. It's Gibberish.

Since they were born, Mae Mae and Bomber have tried to communicate with us through this Gibberish, firmly believing what they were saying made perfect and complete sense to us. It did not.

So as they've grown, we've worked on moving them from Gibberish to English.

At about sixteen months of age, Mae Mae's English vocabulary consisted of about twenty words (but twice as many animal sounds). The words were English in origin, but they didn't quite sound that way. "Help, please" sounded like "hairpiece." "Doh" could've meant "dog," or it could've meant any animal at all that exists in the universe. "Side" meant, "Let's take a walk outside so that I can see all the dohs."

Our goal was to help Mae Mae move toward English and away from Gibberish, which is, like Latin, a dead language.

The process was slow and sometimes frustrating. When Mae Mae used her words to tell us what she was thinking, feeling, or wanting, it went easily. When she couldn't quite get it right, it'd upset her. Through the successes and through the failures, though, Mae Mae was learning. She was learning what made sense and what didn't make sense. She was learning to communicate more clearly and effectively.

If I were suddenly forced to learn to talk at my current age, I can see that being a wildly frustrating endeavor. For instance, I can't imagine learning to speak a new language at this age. ("Look at that . . . *gato* . . . or is it *perro*? I can't remember which one means 'bird' and which one means 'horse.'")

Mae Mae, though, never seemed to get too rattled about the whole process. In fact, she seemed to like it.

Strike that. Mae Mae loved learning.

When we'd teach her a new word, she'd smile and say it back to us. Then again. Then again. Then again and again and again.

She'd try the word out in different contexts. Sometimes she'd get it right ("Yes, honey, that *is* a raisin!"), and sometimes she'd get it wrong ("No, sweetie, a cow says 'moo,' not 'pfffftttt.'"). No matter, she was always game for the process.

And the process made her smile. And laugh. Even when it was hard and she didn't get it, she'd figure it out and come to that same place of smiling and laughing.

I wish I was more like Mae Mae as God grows things in me. I wish I wasn't so consumed with the end result and was, instead, happy to be with my Father, working on something, going through the highs and the lows. I wish I appreciated the process.

I don't think the growth process was meant to feel like drudgery. I actually think it's meant to feel like the opposite. I think when we have the right perspective and we trust God and His love for us and believe He has good things for us, even in the midst of the growth, then we get something deep and beautiful and wonderful.

I think we get joy.

Appreciating the process makes growth more fun and productive.

THE TALKING FIELD

When Mae Mae was only three, she started to figure out how to read. We're not parental tyrants, pushing her to read at a young age. She just seemed to love the process. So my wife and I worked with her on sight words, teaching her how to write, spell, and identify words that show up in the books she loves.

After her sister went down for a nap, Mae Mae would turn to me or my wife and say, "Can we do my sight words now, please? Please?!" Then we'd go to the kitchen table with a stack of flashcards, a few crayons, some paper, and a book or two. After twenty minutes, she'd have learned a word like *they* or *seven* or *gubernatorial.*

Here's how this whole "learning to read" thing did *not* play out:

Me: *Learn to read, Mae Mae.*

Mae: *Okay.*

Then she went to her room and learned to read by herself.

Instead, her learning to read happened when she and I (or she and her mommy) worked on it together. Talking the whole way through, identifying what's happening, asking lots of questions, and even being grateful for the process.

Working with clients, I often find I become friends with them in the process. We work hard, but we also joke around, connect over common interests or life stages, and get to know each other in some pretty deep and meaningful ways. A camaraderie emerges in the thick of the battle to help them become a better speaker. That wouldn't happen if I just gave my clients a copy of *Jeff's Guide to Talking Better and Sounding Gooder on Stage* and told them to improve.

As we take part in the growth process, God doesn't want us taking our assignments to our mental bedrooms to work on them alone. In fact, I think He hates that kind of thing.

He wants us communicating all of the way through the process with Him.

That means we ask Him questions, talk with Him about the insights we're gaining, converse about wins and losses, and even express gratitude to Him for what's going on.

On my perseverance journey, I've found I'm prone to go it alone. To take my orders from God ("*For Your Eyes Only*: Jeff, become perseverant. That is all."), salute Him, then get to doing what I need to be doing.

That's not relationship. That's living less like a friend and more like a slave.

The best times in this perseverance process have been when I've prayed to God, talking with Him about how things are going. They've been the times when I've marveled at how far I've come, even though it hasn't always been an easy process. They've been when I've asked Him what He's up to—even if I don't always receive a clear answer. They've been those quiet, subtle moments when—without a lot of fanfare—I've just said something like, "Thanks for growing perseverance in me. This is really good, I think," while I was driving in my car.

I know I'm more likely to stick with the entire process if I remind myself it is something I'm doing with my friend, Jesus. I'll keep going if I can express frustration and disappointment while also celebrating wins with Him.

I know fields can't talk, but imagine they could. Imagine a field saying something like: "This is great. Now, why did you plow it west-to-east and not north-to-south? Man, this is gonna be a long process, but a good one. I'm looking forward to soybeans! Thanks, Farmer. You're great at this."

It's good for us to talk with God during this growth process. He loves it and . . . it's really good for us.

When we see the growth process as a part of relationship with God, we can delight in it like God does.

COOL YOUR HEELS

Sometimes the thing we need to do is to *not* do.

Sometimes we need to cool our heels.

(Isn't that a great phrase, "Cool your heels"? It just means, "You've been going hard. Sit down. Put your feet up and let those heels that got so hot from you rushing, rushing, rushing all round get some air on 'em." I like using the phrase because it makes me feel like I'm a tough guy in the 1940s wearing a striped suit and flipping a coin to pass the time.)

What if we never stopped working, working, working? What could happen? Here are two possible outcomes:

We'd push through, get to the end, and think, "Well, I sure did it! Yes, I did! I did it! All me! Yahoo, me!" and we'd totally cut God out of the whole thing.

We'd get so exhausted we'd fall over. And, having fallen over, we'd give up staying with our part in the growth process.

Neither is good. The first one is a total illusion because we're never truly going to accomplish good growth in us without God. The second one kills us—and it happens more often than the first.

Back in the early days of God's chosen people, Israel, God made it clear they weren't meant to work and work and work without a break. He knew it would destroy them if they did, and He knew all their efforts could confuse them into thinking they were ultimately responsible for bringing good things to themselves.

So God instituted the Sabbath. The Sabbath was—and is—a day when the people who follow God don't do any work.

It wasn't meant to be a hyper-strict, religious, controlling mandate.

It was actually meant to be a delight to the people. Something that brought them ease and rest.

We need Sabbaths in our tending process. This may not be a one-day-a-week-I'm-going-to-rest-from-the-tending-process situation. It could be more of a season. Without some sort of Sabbath, we'll burn out by constantly challenging ourselves and working toward growth.

Sometimes we're not meant to do anything.

And when we practice the discipline of not doing anything, we actually remind ourselves we're not the ones ultimately on the hook for our growth.

It's God. God's the one who does it.

Jesus said it like this:

> This is what the kingdom of God is like. A man scatters seed on the ground. Night and day, whether he sleeps or gets up, the seed sprouts and grows, though he does not know how. All by itself the soil produces grain—first the stalk, then the head, then the full kernel in the head. As soon as the grain is ripe, he puts the sickle to it, because the harvest has come.
>
> —Mark 4:26–29

Wait . . . someone doesn't do any work—the lazy dude sleeps in!—yet the seed grows? How does that work?

It works because God is working. God is doing. God's making the good stuff happen.

I love this passage even though it seems to fly in the face of us taking part in the process because it's a good reminder that it all comes back to the One Who Is Behind the Scenes. He makes it all happen.

When I rest, I remind myself He's doing the stuff, not me really.

Does Bomber empty the dishwasher? Not really. I do. I take the plates from her and put them where they're meant to go. I move the forks she's placed in the wrong place to where they belong. I restack the bowls.

She's a part of it, but I'm making sure it's done.

The benefit of this is that the pressure is off Bomber to really get it all right. She can try and fail and have fun doing it because I'm gonna make sure it gets done.

On my perseverance journey, I do things to tend the seed, but I also rest sometimes.

I recently decided to take one day a week off from a big writing project I've been doing in an effort to remind myself the perseverance it's producing isn't meant to be the result of all my working—it's the result of God and what He's doing behind the scenes.

Taking that day off also helps me pace myself. It keeps me from burning out when I'm just a few days or weeks into the process.

Ask anybody who knows anything about muscles and how they grow (someone besides me), and they'll tell you that though it would seem to reason the more days you work out the faster your muscles will grow, in fact, without a rest day, those muscles aren't going to get bigger—they're going to get hurt.

My Sabbath days let my perseverance muscle recover, keeping me on the path longer.

And isn't that what we want more of—"a long obedience in the same direction" (to borrow a phrase from Eugene Peterson who borrowed it from Frederick Nietzsche).

Doing is important. Rest is too.

MICKLES AND MUCKLES

When it's not a time or season of rest, I've found the most helpful way of considering my part in the growth process is thinking in terms of mickles and muckles.

This comes from an old Scottish saying: Many a mickle makes a muckle.

It's a colorful way of saying, "Lots of little things combine to make one big thing."

Elements of the process to grow perseverance in me have been muckles—big things.

⊙ Committing to write *Tour Dates*
⊙ Working out for six weeks without giving up
⊙ Sticking with a new job

Those are big "chores" and things that require quite a bit of effort.

But on a day-to-day basis, those muckles were only accomplishable if they were looked at as smaller elements within those larger elements. To make a muckle, I had to focus on the individual mickles that make up a muckle.

You don't "go the gym for six weeks" all at once. That's a muckle. Instead, you do a bunch of mickles like: putting your shoes on, driving your car to the gym, loading up a podcast, running for one minute, then running for another minute, then another, then another, then going home and showering.

Writing *Tour Dates* wasn't about the muckle—writing 120 pages—it was about the mickle—writing one thousand sentences.

Sticking with a new job at a new company wasn't about working there for over a year. It was about showing up at 8:00 a.m. on a Monday. Then on a Tuesday. Then on a Wednesday.

And honestly this book you're reading is the result of lots of little things. This book didn't suddenly appear out of thin air. It came about because, for a whole lot of mornings, I got up at 5:00 a.m. and wrote from 5:30–7:30 before I played with the girls, grabbed a shower, and headed to work. A book is a muckle. Getting up and writing for an hour or two is a mickle.

There's something in our culture that recognizes massive, big achievements as single, Herculean efforts. We rarely notice they're actually comprised of a billion smaller achievements.

My body looks like a unified whole, but it is, in fact, made up of about 37 trillion tiny cells.

Neil Armstrong got this when he recognized the "giant leap for mankind" was, in fact, "one small step for man," which, in turn, was the last moment in a long series of moments that included thousands of math equations, hundreds of slide rules, and millions of spent nerd brain cells.

I took on a speaker coaching client who, at first glance, seemed like a lost cause. She was as dynamic as a dial tone and as comfortable as a cat in a roomful of rocking chairs. I wasn't the only one who realized how hard it was going to be to get her to improve—she felt it too. But I'd seen hard cases before, and I knew it would just take time. She didn't realize that, though. So at the end of the first session, when she didn't sense much improvement, she wanted to bail. In fact, when it came time for our next meeting, she figured out a way to get out of it. She did it with our rescheduled slot too. Eventually, though, we had that second meeting. I began our session by telling her the only way she'd ever really improve was if she focused less on the giant task at hand (her improvement) and, instead, focused on *that single session* and doing what I asked her to in that session. When that happened, she started to improve. Not a ton but enough . . . for her to show up at the next session. And the next. And the next. I'm happy to say that after a few months of regular meetings, with her focusing on small steps rather than the whole journey, she's become a more powerful speaker.

In the Old Testament Book of Zechariah, God talks to the nation of Israel about how they're viewing a massive public works project. "Everybody wants the Temple rebuilt. Everybody wants it done. But, when it comes down to it, y'all aren't as excited about doing the little things to get it done." He says it this way: "Who dares despise the day of small things?" (Zechariah 4:10).

That thought goes through my mind all the time. I think about how I want big things to be done, but I don't seem to want to do the small things to get the big thing done. I love the idea of a finished project, but I despise doing the small things to make it happen.

I want to be a loving husband, but I'm not so jazzed about filling the gas tank in her car at 11:00 p.m. because my wife needs to go somewhere in the morning and forgot the Honda's gonna be thirsty.

I want to be a good friend, but often the idea of leaving the comfort of my couch and Netflix outweighs driving through traffic to meet up with someone.

I want to be a praying person, but I don't really actually want to—you know—pray.

If I want big things growing in my field, I have to think of them as the sum of a lot of small things.

If I want a muckle, I need a bunch of mickles.

However I'm not saying that because they're small little mickles they'll be easy to do. They won't, necessarily. Sometimes those small steps will require a lot from you.

A little act of faith can sometimes require a lot of your emotion, your humility, and your trust.

A few years into our marriage we discovered my wife had this kind of wonky health thing going on. It's wasn't life-ending or anything, but when we found out about it, it rattled us both.

We weren't ready to have kids yet, but the wonky health thing called the idea of having children into question. We both started to wonder: "Will it just be us for the rest of our lives? No kids?" That was very, very hard on both of us.

But then God started to communicate some things to us— that, yes, we would have kids and all would be well.

That didn't sound logical to us. It sounded like a silly fantasy. It sounded like the musings of someone who had lost their mental faculties and was just trying to hear what they wanted to hear.

Still, this idea kept coming back to us—in times we'd spend praying, reading the Bible, talking together. And it also came to us through close friends who saw our broken hearts. I distinctly remember Kristin and I eating dinner with one friend at an outdoor restaurant. Our friend wanted to tell us something she'd felt God had told her. With tears just sitting on that little ledge at the bottom of her eyes, she said, "I keep feeling like— over and over again—God is telling me, 'This health problem will not affect Jeff and Kristin's children.'" When she said that, I broke down crying, and I seem to remember Kristin getting choked up too. This word felt like something coming from God—and something more than just what we wanted to hear.

We stored this word we were receiving through multiple sources in our hearts, reminding each other of it and drawing hope from it.

A couple of years later, it seemed as though the wonky health thing had gone away. We were so relieved. With it fading in our rearview mirror, we started to feel freer to talk about going down the road of starting to have children.

Around that time, I was asked to speak at an event in Norway (I know! Norway!) and was able to bring Kristin along with me. This also happened to be near our five-year anniversary, so we decided to parlay the trip into an anniversary/new season of life celebration by tacking on a weekend in Paris. Our thought was that a few days in France would be perfect for toasting five strong marital years and discussing our vision for a family and what steps we'd need to take to increase our crew from two to more.

After my speaking engagement ended, we flew from Oslo to Paris. We headed straight for a beautiful little boutique hotel we'd booked, dropped off our bags, and went to see the city. In a period of twelve hours, we ate at two different sidewalk cafés, experienced the grandeur of Notre-Dame, covered half the acreage of the Louvre, climbed the steps of Montmartre, and looked out on the Eiffel Tower and the Paris city lights from Sacré-Cœur. We hardly ever stopped in those twelve hours except to turn to each other and say, "Can you believe we're here?" or "Can you believe we've been married five years?" or "Can you believe, maybe some time soon, it won't just be the two of us? Maybe soon we'll have kids?"

It was well past midnight when we made it back to our hotel room. We were both invigorated but also exhausted, having taken in so much of the city. We collapsed into our bed, smiling widely, excited at the beautiful trip God had given us, the new season that lay ahead, and the next day when we were going to go to a fancy restaurant to officially celebrate our marriage and the new family we'd be starting.

Then, without going into details, we awoke the next morning with a shock: the awful, terrible, wonky health thing had returned. This health thing that hadn't shown its face in some time had come back, that morning—the morning of the day we'd set aside to celebrate and imagine.

I'm not sure that *devastating* is a strong enough word.

I remember it was gray and cold and raining that morning. The clouds dropped like a giant, heavy wet glove over the city. And over us. We felt crushed.

We tried to talk each other out of the emotional and spiritual hole we were in, but it felt like no use.

Eventually we made our way to the hotel's restaurant for breakfast. We'd been looking forward to having authentic French croissants for months. We both picked at what was set before us, hardly eating anything.

We didn't know what to do. We stared at each other. We stared off. Our minds and our souls went off in a thousand depressing directions. We asked ourselves and each other answerless questions like, "What does this mean? Is this going to take over our lives?" and, the most pressing of all, "Are we ever going to have children?"

After an eternity of really, just kind of sitting there, we decided to get up from the table and go somewhere. We chose a museum across town. Sure. Why not?

With our coats pulled up tight and my arm around Kristin's shoulder, we walked out into the city on a rainy, dead, Sunday morning in Paris.

We hardly talked as we moved along the sidewalks, our heads down. The Paris of the night before—alive and full of people—now seemed numb and empty. Kind of like us.

After a few moments, though, we saw a line of people. These people were well dressed and holding big books, headed into an old building (which are pretty common in Paris). We realized all of these folks were carrying Bibles, walking into a church. This was surprising to us. We'd always heard that the city of cathedrals was actually pretty dead toward religion and God. We thought it an anomaly and kept going.

A few blocks later, at a different church, we saw the same thing. Lots of people—old and young—gathering in the drizzle outside a cathedral, ready to go inside for worship.

And a few blocks later, more of the same.

You may think something like this might have, in that moment, inspired my faith or given me a spiritual shot in the arm. But, to be honest, it didn't. In fact, just the thought of God made me angry. Why had this happened? And why had this happened on this morning of all mornings? Why had He allowed us to have hope? Why had He convinced us that things were "okay"? Why had He given us a sense—a word—that we would, indeed, have kids?

I gritted my teeth and we kept walking.

Walking, walking, walking.

And all the while, something kept nagging inside of me.

Maybe *nagging* isn't the word. Maybe *nudging* is.

Something inside me was nudging me toward something I did not want to go toward.

Something inside me was nudging me toward . . . belief. Trust. Hope.

I didn't want those things. Or, rather, I didn't want to allow myself to give into those things. I didn't want to be fooled again. I didn't want to be disappointed again. And I didn't want either of those things for Kristin either.

I could feel the beginning of some sort of callous forming over my heart and soul.

I tried to shut the nudging out.

But it just . . . kept . . . nudging me.

Imagine a house on fire. Now imagine a small child trapped in their second story bedroom. Imagine the child is at the window, crying out. Now imagine a ladder leans against the outside of the home. A firefighter climbs the ladder. He's right outside the child's window. He wants the child to take the small step from the windowsill into his arms. The child doesn't want to do it. The step—twenty feet up from the sill to the firefighter—seems illogical and frightening. The firefighter could shout at the child, but he knows that may only scare the child all the more. So instead, in the midst of the raging, roaring, consuming inferno, he calmly, evenly, serenely says, "It's okay. Just take the step. I know it's hard. But, please, trust me."

In that moment, as we walked, I felt God's voice in just that way inside of me.

Then something inside of me decided: though it's illogical and humiliating and frightening, I needed to take a step.

I looked at the shops lining the sidewalk. I was looking for one particular specialty shop. I had no idea whether or not I'd find one. And, not only that, it was Sunday morning, which meant almost every single shop in the city was closed.

Except one.

Right there in front of us.

And it was the exact type of shop I was looking for.

With my arm around her shoulder, I pulled Kristin closer to me, then to a stop. I looked at the shop. She looked at the shop. "Let's go in here," I said.

After a moment's hesitation, we did.

It was a baby boutique.

Though it was Parisian, it looked like every other baby boutique you've ever seen. Clothes for infants, play toys, stuffed animals.

Doing my best to hold back a whole lot of emotion, I looked Kristin in the eyes and said, "Let's pick something out. An outfit or something. We'll buy it . . . by faith."

If there was any feeling of, "What are you saying? Are you crazy?" inside of Kristin, it lasted for only a split second. After that, she began looking through the stacks of clothing.

Within a minute, she found an all-white, soft-as-a-lamb's-ear zip-up outfit. "This," she said, simply.

Then I saw a small brown blanket with a bunny attacked to one end. I picked it up. "And this."

We walked to the register, side by side.

The cashier smiled at us. "Are you expecting?" she said in French-tinged English.

I wish I remembered exactly what I said in response, but I think it was something along the lines of, "One day."

I also cannot remember exactly how much we paid for that outfit and that blanket. All I know is that when the total came up on the register—and I did the currency conversion—it was a lot.

But it didn't matter. This was our little, tiny act of faith. This was us, taking a tiny step that said to ourselves and to God, "We still have some hope." This was us, buying items for a baby that didn't yet exist.

This was our Parisian mickle.

It wasn't all roses and periwinkles after that. As a matter of fact, it got even tougher for us as more things hit that further called into question our having children.

179

But God stayed with us. And our friends stayed with us. And we stayed with each other. And then . . .

A couple years later, we took Charlotte Mae Davenport home from the hospital in that French outfit. And, two years later, Juliette Scott Davenport came home from the hospital in that outfit too.

And, to this day, Mae Mae sleeps with that bunny.

I know that everyone's it's-hard-for-us-to-get-pregnant stories don't turn out the same. The point, really, isn't us having children.

The point is, in that moment on that French sidewalk, it was important for us to take a tiny step of faith. It was important for us to turn belief into symbolic action to keep the word God had placed within us alive.

Oftentimes small steps add up to the greatest growth.

RESULTS AND ROSES

It's good for us to remind ourselves of what God is growing in us.

It's good for us to share that information with friends so they can support us.

It's good for us to be vigilant, keeping an eye open toward the enemy's lies.

It's good for us to enjoy the process with God, our friend.

It's good for us to rest.

It's good for us to see our parts of the process in smaller, bite-sized pieces.

If we want what God is growing in us, we have to do what we're meant to do—or not do—in the process.

Let's end this with a poem from Edgar Guest called "Results and Roses":

The man who wants a garden fair,
Or small or very big,
With flowers growing here and there,
Must bend his back and dig.
The things are mighty few on earth
That wishes can attain.
Whate'er we want of any worth
We've got to work to gain.
It matters not what goal you seek
Its secret here reposes:
You've got to dig from week to week
To get Results or Roses.

Three Questions

Who's one person you can talk with about what you believe God is growing in you?

How can you break up the "muckle" God is growing into daily "mickles"?

What does rest look like for you, in the midst of God growing good things?

Chapter 8
The Waiting

Even youths grow tired and weary, and young men stumble and fall; but those who hope in the LORD will renew their strength. They will soar on wings like eagles; they will run and not grow weary, they will walk and not be faint.

—Isaiah 40:30–31

A businessman who lives in town passes the Farmer's land on his drive to work each day.

The businessman doesn't think much of the field. To him, it just looks like dirt. A big patch of nothing.

One day as he passes the field, the businessman's car gets a flat tire.

From a few acres away, the Farmer notices. Handy with a tire iron and always looking to do a kindness, the Farmer puts down his shovel and heads over to the businessman and his car.

"Give you a hand?" the Farmer asks.

"That'd be great," the businessman says.

As the Farmer works the flat, the businessman looks out at the field.

"You know," the businessman says, "this plot of land you've got here could be turned over into a nice little commercial center. A few shops on that end, maybe a bank over there . . ."

The Farmer keeps working the tire and says, "Naw. I'm growing things on this here land."

"Oh," the businessman says as he looks over at the land, wiping sweat from his eyes. A slightly confused look crosses his face.

The Farmer notices. He stands. Points to the land, grinning. *"Over there, that's for apple trees. Apples so sweet your dentist will get mad at you for eating 'em. And over there, tomatoes so red, you'll think they're stoplights. And just beyond them, roses so bright you'll have to shade your eyes just to get a look at 'em."*

The businessman doesn't see anything of the sort. All he sees is dirt. Acres and acres of dirt, spotted with the occasional tiny green leaf or skinny stem. *"Well, I'm sorry, sir, but . . ."* The businessman pauses, choosing his words carefully, so as not to imply the Farmer is crazy—though that's what the businessman is thinking. *"I guess I don't see anything out there."*

The Farmer kneels back down to the tire, removing the final lug nut. *"You will,"* he says. *"Soon enough."*

The businessman shakes his head and rolls the spare toward the Farmer.

Day after day, the businessman passes the field on his way into and out of town. Some days he sees the Farmer out doing chores. Other days he sees him sitting out on his porch, drinking lemonade and eyeing the field. The businessman never seems to see anything growing though.

A few weeks after the flat, the businessman stops of his own accord at the field. Walks out toward the Farmer who's pulling up a bit of kudzu.

"You wanna give a second thought to selling this land, sir?"

The Farmer chuckles—not in an insulting way, but in an amused way.

I AM A FIELD

"I could give you, say, $150 an acre—"

"Thank you, sir, but I'm happy with what I got."

"Sir—"the businessman stammers, "—for weeks I've been driving by here, and there's nothing out there. No apple trees. No roses. No tomatoes. Just dirt! Nothing but dirt! Are you off your nut?"

"Have a good day, sir," the Farmer says as he turns his attention to a tiny weed.

The businessman shakes his head as he heads back toward his car. "I hope you know what you're doing."

"I do," the Farmer says, digging into the dirt. "I'm waiting," he says without looking up.

The businessman rolls his eyes. Climbs into his car with a sigh. "Well, good luck with that."

"Thank you," the Farmer says.

As the businessman drives away, the Farmer looks back out at the field. Yup, it just looks like a lot of dirt with little evidence of growth.

But that's okay.

The Farmer knows everything's going to grow up just like he'd planned.

He just has to tend . . . and wait.

CUCUMBERS AND BAMBOO

If you want to grow your own cucumber in a garden, it's going to take about seven weeks for that cucumber seed to turn into something you can chop up and drop into a salad.

Corn? Corn can take around three months. Three months until sweet yellow niblets start popping up on the ears.

Apple seed takes anywhere from six to ten years to go from Johnny Appleseed's cast-off to a fruit-bearing tree.

184

Kale takes two months for the ground to infuse it with that delicious Windex-and-sweat flavor all those healthy kooks have come to love.

The fastest growing plant in the world is bamboo. It can grow up to 35 inches a day. That may seem fast, but if a bamboo plant had a speedometer, it would read about 0.00002 miles per hour. If you drove a car that speed, you'd think it was still in park.

Whether it's cucumbers or corn or bamboo, a time of waiting is required to grow something good.

You can't get around it.

If you try to short circuit the slow-growing process—using chemicals or modifications to speed things along—you end up with weird, ersatz crops like a square tomato or pears with the skin on the inside or watermelons the size of end tables. Those "foods" probably aren't good for you—or anyone else.

Real, life-giving crops only come about after a time of waiting.

It's the same with the things God is growing inside of us. They take time to grow. A time of waiting.

Could God grow a carrot in seventeen seconds? He sure could. And, I assume, for some reason or another, He has. (Maybe as a quiet, out-of-the-way miracle for a hungry jackrabbit in the Mojave Desert.)

Could God grow good things inside of us in the blink of an eye? Yes. He sure could. In fact, I've heard stories of people who've been suddenly rescued from bad habits and temptations in a moment. Crazy stories.

It's been my experience, though—and the experience of most of the people I've talked to—that God's typical *modus operandi* is to grow things slowly, over time.

But why does He allow it to take time?

(If you're currently in a season of waiting, you may ask that question in a different way. More like, "Why in the blooming world does God let things take so flippy-gallippy long? I mean, seriously! Also, what does flippy-gallippy mean? I'm so frustrated and confused!")

I believe one reason God allows growth to take time is He wants to go through the process alongside of us, living out our friendship as we go. If He just snapped His celestial fingers and—*blammo*—we suddenly had the thing He (and we) wanted grown in us, there wouldn't be much time or opportunity to go through the process with Him. Remember me emptying the dishwasher together with Bomber? I could've done it alone in 88.7 seconds (I've timed myself), but when I do it with her, I get to have fun with her, accomplishing something with her and connecting with her.

Another reason I believe God allows growth to take time is that, as humans, we typically prize and more highly value those things that come after a season of waiting. Think about the time you saved your allowance up for something when you were a kid. Think about when you were engaged for six long months. Think about the vacation you were looking forward to taking. If you suddenly got the toy or ran off and eloped or found yourself on a plane to Hawaii, you may not value those things as much. When we work and wait and what we've hoped for finally comes about, we're more likely to appreciate it.

I know, I know, I know. Even with those reasons, I know it's hard to wait. Believe me. I'm one of the worst in the world about waiting.

How many grilled cheese sandwiches have I eaten that were charred black on the outside but had unmelted cheese inside because I'd turned up the heat on the frying pan as high as it could go to get the process done as quickly as possible? (Answer: many.)

How many times have I committed to going to the gym, only to give up after one trip because, upon looking down at my body afterwards, I didn't suddenly look like Ryan Reynolds? (Answer: a whole lot.)

How often have I bailed on cleaning out the basement because it took longer than the minute-and-a-half I apparently thought it should take? (Answer: let's just say that if it weren't for my wife, our basement would look like a candidate for FEMA disaster recovery.)

The old cliché is we live in a microwave culture: we want our frozen burrito hot now. Thirty seconds? Too long. Faster. Faster. Faster. We won't be satisfied until that burrito is cooked the moment it emerges from the freezer.

Part of the process of growing something inside of us is God growing patience too. Patience is a side crop that grows well as a companion to other crops. It's like growing basil—a natural insect deterrent—beside tomatoes. Without basil, the tomatoes won't make it. Without patience, and the other things God's trying to grow in us, we won't grow well either.

I had a wise friend tell me, "God's always on time. He's rarely early . . . but He's always on time." That made me laugh when she'd say it because I knew in my bones it was true—and it also drove me a little nuts. Rarely in my life has something I've been waiting on come sooner than I'd expected. Usually it took longer to arrive.

When we're aware of the fact that time is required to grow good things—and come to terms with that—we can let the process fully play out and actually, possibly, enjoy the process. Just knowing we have to wait can make things better.

I loathe traffic. To me, it's on par with mosquito bites and when the bottom of your jeans gets stuck behind the tongue of your shoe. (I'm not alone in my hatred of traffic, right? I'm pretty sure everyone hates it. Have you ever heard someone say they liked it? I can't imagine "sitting in traffic" working its way into the lyrics of that "My Favorite Things" song from *The Sound of Music*.)

Now, imagine two scenarios. In the first, you hop in your car, rushing to get to a meeting across town. Usually the trip takes ten minutes. As you pull onto the highway, your heart sinks. It's a total parking lot. No one's moving. You shake your head. Look at your watch. Then you sit there, inching your car forward—bit by bit.

What should have been a ten-minute ride ends up taking twenty-five minutes.

Now, imagine things had played out a bit differently. Imagine you're about to hop into your car for that meeting across town. You know the trip should take ten minutes. But, before you get into your car, you check traffic on your phone. There's lots and lots of traffic. It's going to take longer than you expected.

You get in your car with the knowledge the drive will take a while. In fact it ends up taking you thirty minutes to get there.

Which is a worse scenario? Not expecting traffic, and the drive taking you fifteen minutes longer than it normally would . . . or expecting traffic and the drive taking you twenty minutes longer?

I say the first is worse. Even though it takes less time, it's that shock of, "What?! There's traffic! Now? How is this possible?! Nooooo!" that makes the drive so much more annoying and frustrating.

If I know beforehand that something's going to take a long time, I handle it better. Waiting is still not something I love (like strawberry ice cream with Snickers), but it's more palatable.

We can't enter into the growth process with any illusions. It takes time. If we don't understand that, we will get very, very annoyed and frustrated. Not only that, but it can put the crops in jeopardy.

LET THE BABY GROW

When my cousin was pregnant with her first child, she couldn't wait to meet her little baby. She was so excited, in fact, she had a disturbing recurring dream throughout her pregnancy. In the dream, my cousin was laying in bed, looking at her stomach, wanting to see her baby so badly she figured out a way to pull the baby out—just to get a look at it. Once she'd seen the baby, she tried to put the baby back—but it wouldn't go back. The baby just laid in her arms though it needed to be back in its little womb-oven, cooking until it was done.

Impatience makes us do crazy things—like pulling out babies to get a look at them before they're ready to greet the world (or at least, we dream about things like that).

If we're impatient during the growth process as God grows good things on our field, we'll be prone to respond in ways that won't be good for the crop—and thus won't be good for us or the people around us.

Throughout my life, I've done a lot of waiting—waiting for good things to come along that I believed God was bringing and growing. It's happened so often, I feel like half my life has been spent riding in an airplane that's in a holding pattern, circling an airport.

Sometimes I've responded well during those waiting times. More often than not I haven't responded well.

And when I didn't wait well, I tended to undercut the growth that was meant to be bringing about a crop.

Through my experience, I've identified a few responses I'm prone to have when I'm in a waiting season. These are the responses that keep the good things from coming the way they're meant to come.

Response #1: "I misheard God."

This is a very, very common one for me. I've responded this way so many times, it's almost become a habit. I'll be going along, reminding myself of some word God had given me ("I want to grow perseverance in you!" "You're going to be a father!" "Your marriage is going to get stronger!"), doing what I'm meant to do, tending the field, working the land. And I do well for a while . . . until the process takes longer than I'd expected. So I start to question what I heard in the first place. "Surely God wouldn't let this take so long. And if He wouldn't let it take this long, then I must have made a mistake. I must not have heard Him right the first time."

Imagine you're tending a field and you suddenly decide there was no seed to begin with. You'd originally thought there was seed in the ground, but then you came to the conclusion: "That's crazy. There is no seed down there." Would you keep watering it and protecting it and making sure it got sunshine? No. You wouldn't. Because you wouldn't think there was anything there to begin with. And what would happen then? The seed that was down there—and had been down there all along—wouldn't grow. It would wither away.

During the waiting season, it's natural for us to question ourselves and our abilities to hear from God clearly. We get rattled. We look for someone to blame. And that blame usually lands on us. "If I was more spiritual or something, I might have gotten God's message more clearly. I would've realized a long time ago He wasn't really saying anything to me about perseverance . . . or being a father . . . or my marriage. What was I thinking?"

And when that happens, the seed is in danger.

Response #2: "God lied."

Sometimes the blame we desperately want to place ends up landing on God. So we think He lied to us.

We typically don't explicitly think God lied, but that's behind what we start to feel. We question whether or not He's really going to do what we felt like He said He was going to do. We wonder if He changed His mind, if He's forgotten us, or worse.

The "worse" is when we question the two things at the root of His trustworthiness: His wisdom and His love.

"God lied" usually plays out as, "You don't get it. I need this *now*. This waiting around has to stop. I can't keep going like this. If You really saw all this clearly, you'd know that 'now' is better than 'later.'" Really, we say, "I see the timeline more clearly than You. I'm wiser than You about when the right time is. And the right time is now. You lied when You said You saw this all better than I."

"God lied" also plays out as, "You say You love me? You don't love me. If You really loved me, You wouldn't make me wait." The core attribute of God—His love (1 John 4:8 says,

"God is love.")—is put on trial. The "He loves me/He loves me not" game comes down to a single question: "If You really loved me, why wouldn't You give me this right now? Why would You have me wait?"

I can't tell you how many times I've thought, in some form or fashion, "God's lied to me. He doesn't really love me that much." The thing I love about God the most—His love for me!—gets tossed because I'm having to wait.

I see this in Mae Mae's eyes sometimes when I don't do what she wants me to do right away. Something in her gets panicky and nervous. Deep down, her little brain is trying to make sense of a daddy who shows her he loves her by kissing her, tickling her, wrestling her, telling her he loves her, but won't do what she's wanting him to do for her right at that moment. What she knows deep down—"Daddy loves me"— is offset by her perspective on things—that right now is the best time for something.

When we think God's lied to us—or, at least, misrepresented Himself, His plan, His wisdom, or His love—we give up on the seed. Why bother? "He's not really wise" and "He's not really loving" results in "I don't trust Him. I don't believe Him when He says something good will come in time." And what happens to the seed or plant? It withers.

Response #3: "It's not worth it."

When you're planning to do something, the most important question to ask is, "Will the end result be worth the waiting?"

"Is visiting the Iowa state capitol building worth nine hours in the car with three sweaty, Mountain Dew-slurping, smelly dudes?"

"This movie is three-and-a-half hours. Will I feel satisfied with the story after sitting on my couch watching Al Pacino yell in a New Jersey accent for that long?"

"We're gonna wait forty-five minutes for a table. Is the sushi that good? Is it worth hovering in the bar area for almost an hour?"

Any time I've given up on a project, I've either consciously or unconsciously come to the conclusion that what I was putting into the project wasn't worth what I could possibly get out of it. Which is more valuable to me? Three hours to myself or a clean basement? My mornings spent reading entertainment news or slowly writing a book? Just coasting through my marriage or putting in the effort to show my wife I love her?

When we get to a point where the final outcome doesn't seem worth the waiting, we question why we put the effort in to begin with and, furthermore, question why God would've allowed us to start down this road at all.

This one is based on a pretty simple math equation: if the pain of the waiting period is greater than the perceived value of the good thing coming, then I'm not waiting anymore. I give up.

That may seem cold and stark, but our brains and emotions have a tendency to constantly reassess whether we're going to wait it out on things based on this if/then test.

For instance, if the pain and endurance required to selflessly serve my spouse with the hope she'll recommit to our marriage is greater than how good I think our marriage will be on the other side of the waiting, then I won't want to wait anymore. I'll settle on keeping the marriage the way it is.

If you think the final crop growth will be worth the waiting and the doing and the trying and the patience, you'll stick with it. If you don't, you won't.

When we think we've misheard God, that He lied, or that the waiting isn't worth it (or some combination of those things), the ultimate realization of all of the potential inside the seed gets called into question.

There's rarely a single moment when we fully give up on the seed, though. It rarely happens in an angry, frustrated flash.

More often than not, the death of the seed is slow.

It starts with a little less effort put into its care. A little less watering. A little less sunshine. A little less crow chasing.

With perseverance, I noticed a subtle tendency to stop keeping an eye open to be challenged. A bit of laziness creeping in, more and more. Less talking with God and my friends about what I thought God was growing in me.

Left unchecked, I'd end up not thinking about the seed at all.

And, with that, the chances of that crop growing up in me would be less and less.

I've seen people try to love their spouses better . . . but when it didn't have results as soon as they wanted, they bailed on their marriage.

I've seen people want to become more in touch with God's love for them. But when seeing a fuller realization of that took a long time, they gave up on the pursuit.

I've seen people want God to grow confidence in them, but because it was a lengthy growth period, they went back to their default of self-loathing.

And when all of this happens, the seed dies . . . without ever having produced its fruit.

Thoroughly depressed yet? Well I kind of am.

In lieu of ice cream, let's try to change our perspective a little bit.

GROWING UNDERGROUND

If you were looking at a field that had seed planted in it, how would you know when that seed had started growing? Most of us would probably stand over the place where the seed was planted and watch. And watch. And watch. Finally, after enough watching, a little bit of green would show up on the surface of the dirt. "There!" we'd yell. "The seed is finally growing!"

But anyone who knows anything about seeds knows that's not when the seed started growing. The seed had been growing for days—maybe even weeks—before that.

We didn't see it because the growth was happening underground.

Let's say a seed is three inches beneath the earth's surface. When that seed begins to grow into something more than just an oval pod, a little stem-y thing (not a horticultural term) comes out of it. A lot of the time, that stem-y thing goes out from the side or from the bottom—not even from the top. It grows and grows, poking around the soil for a while, until finally it aims toward the surface. Then it makes the long trek up to fresh air.

This part of the process can take a while.

When we stand over the ground, looking down, thinking nothing's happening, we're actually fooling ourselves. In fact, we're being arrogant. Our arrogance is a result of us thinking we have the best vantage point for making the call on whether or not a seed is growing.

Our vantage point isn't as good as it would be if we could, somehow, be under the earth, watching that seed crack open and the stem-y thing poke out. From that vantage point, we'd see that the underground growth is actually the beginnings of a root system that will eventually be vitally important to the plant—keeping it anchored in the earth as well as able to receive the nutrients from the soil it needs to grow.

But we can't see down there, can we?

Most of the time when God's growing things in us—while we're waiting—we can't tell what's going on right away. We can't see what's going on underground. We just stand on the surface, looking down, and we lose heart when we don't see signs of growth . . . or not enough growth for the time we've been waiting.

Waiting—and believing something's happening even when we can't see it—requires faith.

Faith.

If you read the Bible, you see, over and over again, that faith is necessary to follow Jesus.

Why?

Because, put simply, we can't see Jesus. He's not walking around on earth, chatting it up with us at the local coffee shop, going on a run with us, or sitting in the car next to us in rush hour traffic.

I mean, He's doing all of those things in a spiritual sense . . . but in a corporeal, physical sense? No. We can't see Him, smell Him, or touch Him like we can with a regular, human friend.

So what does it take to follow someone you can't see?

It takes faith.

And what does it take to not just follow that person but to let them grow good things in us?

Even more faith.

Here's a great definition of faith from the Bible that lines up with us not being able to see the seed from our spot on the surface: "Now faith is confidence in what we hope for and assurance about what we do not see" (Hebrews 11:1).

It struck me a long time ago that being a farmer must be the most faith-based occupation in the world. A farmer has to trust that if he does some pretty crazy things—dig a hole in dirt, drop a tiny thing into that dirt, water the dirt, sprinkle some animal doo-doo on the dirt, let the sun hit the dirt, then wait—something will happen in a place he can't even see (underground). If he does those things long enough, and waits long enough, *food* will come up out of the ground. That just seems insane.

Waiting and believing something is happening in a realm we can't see seems insane.

Faith seems insane.

And yet it's what we need to let God do what He's going to do in us.

We need faith.

How do you get more faith?

I often look at myself and think, "Well, Self. You need faith. And you don't seem to have much. So work harder at having faith." And do you know how that ends? It ends poorly because we all know you can't just manufacture faith.

Here's something that's freed me up in the times when I can't see what God's doing in the growth process and I'm frustrated and know I need to have faith, but I just don't feel like I have any: "Faith . . . is the gift of God" (Ephesians 2:8).

That Scripture takes the pressure off me. It makes me less concerned about trying, working, and sweating until I suddenly have the faith I need. Faith is a gift. It's something God gives.

So instead of getting a spiritual hernia trying to effort out some faith, I can just ask God to give it to me.

And, I've found, He often does.

Why? Because He knows I need it. He knows I need faith to keeping going, believing He is who He says He is and He's going to do what He said He will do. He knows I need faith to believe growth is happening even when I can't see it. He knows I need faith to wait . . . and to wait well.

God's a good father who gives us what we need. And we need faith.

So if you want more faith, don't try to work it up. Ask your Daddy for it.

STAYING WITH THE SEED

Besides changing our perspective and asking for faith during the process, what else can we do to wait well? Here are a seven things I've found to be helpful:

#1 Get honest with God.

For some reason, I rarely feel as close to God as when I'm facedown in the dirt, honest and gritty with Him. When I'm frustrated and want to give up, I usually go for a drive. While I'm driving, I turn off the music, slap my hand on the steering wheel, and say something (aloud) like, "God! Man! This is not fun! At all! I don't want to keep going. I want to give up. This doesn't seem worth it. And, honestly, I'm not feeling like You're showing any love to me in this. I just don't feel it. I'm starting to wonder if just going back to the old way of doing things isn't the best thing. *Ahhhh!* I don't like this!" Then I hit the steering wheel a couple more times.

When I do this, I do what David did in the Psalms: I vent my spleen. I let out the stuff that's bottled up inside me. I sidestep any sort of shame I may subconsciously be feeling about not wanting to keep going. I just lay it all out.

Sometimes when I do this, I don't get much back from God. No new insights or wisdom. Yet there's something in me that feels better. I think it has to do with reminding myself God doesn't think I always have to feel tip-top and happy to keep going. And when I lose that pressure, I *like* God a little more. And that makes me trust Him more. And want to keep going a little bit longer. To keep waiting.

But sometimes I do get a small nudge from God. That nudge sort of feels like He's letting me know He understands my frustration and He's proud of me for sticking with the process. The feeling that God's proud of me even though I'm grumpy and want to give up feels pretty good. He's a good friend to me in that way.

#2 Get honest with pals.

I'm usually tempted to tell my buddies things are fine even when they're not. This doesn't help me or my friends. Instead it puts a smokescreen up between us, keeping us from knowing each other and me from getting the encouragement, direction, prayer, and help from them.

My life is better when I tell someone else, like my wife, how I'm feeling. This doesn't mean that every day I wake her up in the morning with a groan and a, "Ugh, honey, this is so hard." That would beat anyone down. But it does mean I tell her how I'm feeling about the process—and the waiting—and pointedly ask her to remind me of what good things will come if I keep going.

Dishonesty or putting up a front clogs the pipe God created between my pals and me to provide the things I need to keep going in the process. Honesty and vulnerability act as spiritual Drano, removing blockages and ensuring the flow of good stuff happens.

#3 Think in time chunks.

At the beginning of this year when I decided to try to go to the gym more often, I realized my old way of thinking of going to the gym just plain didn't work. How did I know it didn't work? I'd gained a lot of weight, didn't feel healthy, and went to the gym only when I needed to pick my wife up from there. The gym was not my jam.

But I wanted it to be my jam. I wanted to be a regular there. I wanted to get in shape, feel better, and challenge my heart to something more than the occasional jolt it got from watching an old Hitchcock thriller or when I changed a lightbulb with wet fingers.

So I thought about all of those people in those DVD infomercials I'd seen (for programs with names like, "P49 Blast X!" "Hippity Hoppity Bunny Dance Party Fit Club," or "The C-3PO Workout for Flat, Metal-Hard Abs") and how they'd show before and after pictures. The before and after pics were usually taken about six weeks apart from each other.

Six weeks.

That seemed like a long time.

But it had also become apparent to me that in order to make any progress when it came to fitness, you had to give it at least six weeks.

I wasn't used to six weeks. I was used to sixty minutes. Sixty minutes of working out (which included driving to and from the gym, changing clothes, drinking water, talking with the person at the front desk, talking to my wife about how I went to the gym, and—oh yeah—a few minutes on the elliptical)—not six weeks.

So I decided to commit to six weeks. I told myself, "If at the end of six weeks, I don't see any results, I'll throw in the nasty smelling sweat towel." No giving up before that. No judging how I looked or felt until the six weeks was over.

I'm happy to say I did it. I stuck with it.

And you know what happened? At the end of six weeks I felt better. I'd lost some weight. I even looked better.

And you know what happened after that?

I kept going. And kept going. And kept going.

And here I am, at week twelve, and I don't see any reason to stop anytime soon.

I just needed to think of the process in terms of chunks of time.

Thinking of muckle-y time chunks in terms of mickle-y time bits works for road trips ("We'll drive another hour then take a break and reassess if we want to keep going."), raising a kid ("We just need to get through this season, then she'll sleep a little better."), and cleaning a basement, ("Let's work until 2:00 and see how far we've gotten. No stopping until then.").

My clients don't become Churchillian speakers if they think in terms of the entire transformation process. They improve when they commit to the single, two-hour session in front of them. Then the next one. Then the next one. Only then do they actually improve enough so they could, possibly, address the English Parliament in wartime.

This focus on the mickle-sized chunks of time rather than the muckle-sized ones helps us as we let God grow good things in us too.

I've told God, "I'll keep going for another two weeks as you grow perseverance in me. I'm not going to talk about giving up until two weeks. Okay? Okay." Or with something in my marriage. Or becoming more hopeful.

That doesn't mean I always see signs of growth in two weeks, but I get another two weeks of tending and waiting under my belt at least. And that forward momentum usually keeps me going beyond those two weeks.

#4 Remember God's goodness.

Have you been through this process before? Have you waited for God to grow something good and, finally, it came about? Remember that. Remind yourself God's been faithful and good to you in the past.

Honestly when I'm tempted to give up and go back to my default, I don't know why I don't remind myself of what God's done in the past more often. I almost feel embarrassed at the fact that I don't do this naturally.

When I remind myself of what God's done in the past, I set my mind on the fact God is not a liar. That God helps keep me on track with what He's saying. That it's worth the waiting. I draw on history to make a conclusion about the present.

Draw on your history. And, heck, draw on the history of others too. Have your friends or family gone through times of tending and waiting only to have God bring something good about? Tell yourself those stories. Let them inform your heart and keep you focused on God and how He really does do good things. Read the Bible and how God showed His faithfulness over and over again to people who waited on Him.

My wife and I help each other remember what God has done in our lives often. When one of us is feeling low, the other chimes in with a gentle reminder that God has delivered something good in the past. Those reminders help so much. Without them, we don't have any history to run on. With them, we realize we're just trusting God to do something similar to what He's done in the past.

Remembering God's past faithfulness gives us enough evidence to believe He'll be faithful again.

#5 Remember why you're waiting.

For our honeymoon, Kristin and I went to Kauai—one of the Hawaiian Islands. Before booking the trip, we'd done a lot of research and came to the firm conclusion that Kauai was going to be the best place to spend the first seven days of our marriage. We knew it was going to be great.

But that flight to Hawaii is long. It's very, very long. You get on the plane excited, but after a few hours, you're looking at your watch thinking, "Couldn't we have gone somewhere closer? Like . . . Walla Walla, Washington?"

Whenever the flight felt too long, we got out a Kauai guidebook we'd purchased. This thing was an "insider's" guide, written by a local, who listed out every great place to eat banana pancakes, chow down sushi, watch the sun come up, hike through the jungle, and grab a photo under a waterfall on the island. The more we looked through the book, the faster the flight seemed to go. (It also prepared us for where we were going.)

When you're waiting for God to grow something great in your life, it's helpful to remind yourself along the way what you're waiting for. Like a teenager who puts up a cutout magazine photo of a car they're saving up for on their bedroom wall, we should be reminding ourselves of the great thing we're waiting for.

If you don't remember what you're waiting for, you'll be a lot less likely to stick with the waiting.

It's also helpful to remember that what you're waiting for isn't necessarily about you. God growing perseverance in your life will be great for you, but it's also going to be great for the people around you—the people who count on you. If God's growing you into a stronger spouse, that's going to obviously be a blessing to the person you're married to. If He's growing you into someone who's more skilled and dedicated to your life's calling, that's probably going to impact lots and lots of people beyond yourself.

So don't just remind yourself of how what comes at the end of waiting will improve your life; remind yourself of the people who you'll impact through what God is doing.

Your life is bigger than just you. Jesus knew that. His closest friends knew that. God wants us to know that too.

#6 Know there's a reason you're waiting.
God doesn't have us sitting around waiting for no good reason. Now, the fact is, a lot of the time we don't get a clear reason for all that waiting. But we can believe God's not a bully, and He's not a jerk. He knows it's good for us to wait for one reason or another. (When we trust He's loving and wise, then we believe He's got a reason—even if we don't know it.)

When I was twenty-five I started to get nervous I wasn't going to get married. (Funny, right? Twenty-five?! Well, I'm from Texas and folks get married *very* young there. "Here's your high school diploma . . . and here's your marriage license.") I talked to God a lot about who I was supposed to marry. I usually sensed God telling me to just hang on and to wait.

So I waited.

And waited.

And waited.

Around the age of thirty-one, I started to get concerned. I still wasn't married. And I kept thinking, "*Why* is God making me wait? He's not doing *anything!* He's just got me sitting here, alone, in time-out. Why, God?"

I didn't get an answer.

Until a few months later. That was when God showed me Kristin. The girl I knew I was going to marry.

A twenty-two-year-old.

Now, let's rewind to when I was twenty-five and starting to get antsy about getting married. What if God had given in and said to me, "Fine! You want to know who you're going to marry? Here's what I want you to do: get on a plane and fly to Seattle. Then, drive to a little town about forty-five minutes south of Seattle. There, you'll find a high school. No, your future wife isn't a teacher there. She's a student. Go to Room 205 where she'll be in algebra class . . ."

That would've been weird to me. And confusing. And, probably, disheartening. And illegal.

Having me wait wasn't an arbitrary decision for God. There was a reason behind it. He didn't want me marrying a sixteen-year-old.

Remember there's a reason for the waiting. We don't always know the reason, but God does. And when we trust Him, we trust His reasons for the waiting.

#7 Tell yourself about the waiting.

Again, when you expect traffic, the traffic is less likely to grind you down than when it catches you unaware.

When you're waiting, tell yourself, "Yep. This was to be expected. Waiting is a part of this. There's no getting away from waiting."

Really, you're telling yourself that what you're experiencing isn't an anomaly. When you feel as though something's an anomaly, you freak out and want to bail. But if you're expecting it, you feel a little better. "Well, this means I'm on the right track."

Waiting *is* a part of this process. Know that. If you're waiting, good stuff is surely coming. You don't know when it will come, but don't let yourself get derailed because of the waiting. It's how God functions. And He's with you in the midst of the waiting.

If you've never read Henry Wadsworth Longfellow's great poem, "A Psalm of Life," you're missing out. It's an encouragement to live life to the full—even though it can sometimes be difficult. The poem ends with a great description of how we're meant to keep going:

Still achieving, still pursuing,
Learn to labor and to wait.

Learn seems to be the key word there. We need to learn to do the work, but we also need to learn to wait for the good to come. God helps us with that learning, if we're willing to sit with him on the porch and wait.

A few years ago, I saw a counselor because I was being wracked by fear. Some stuff had happened to my wife and me in the previous months that had rattled me to no end. It made it to where I couldn't sleep at night. I was nervous, worried, and, honestly, scared of the dark. It was all very strange and upsetting and was about to kill me. So I went to see a counselor.

I told the guy, "I've got a fear thing. I'm scared of all sorts of stuff. And it's keeping me from living the life I think God wants me to live." At the end of our first meeting he asked me, "So what do you want from our time together?" I started crying when I answered him: "I just want to get better." He smiled a reassuring smile at me and said, "You will, Jeff. You will."

But the thing is: I didn't get better.

Well, let me correct that: I didn't get better after that meeting.

I slept terribly that next week. I jumped at the slightest noise. I ran up the steps when the lights were off. My hands shook.

But I went back the next week. And he counseled me (as counselors do).

But I didn't get better.

This happened the following week.

Then the following week.

And it seemed as though nothing was happening.

I started to get frustrated because this wasn't what I'd pictured. I'd pictured that after one or two meetings, I'd be sleeping like a log, going to haunted houses for fun, ice climbing thousand-foot-tall frozen waterfalls, and picking fights with Samoan linebackers.

But nope. That wasn't happening.

I wanted to give up. I wanted to stop going to see the guy. I wanted to stop thinking about it all, focusing on my fears, and wrestling with them.

I wanted to stop waiting.

But for a number of reasons—including encouragement from God and from others—I kept at it.

A few weeks later . . . I had one good night's sleep. Not, like, all night. Just a few hours.

But it was better than I'd slept in the prior six months.

And then, a week later, I found myself walking through a dark room at a normal, non-frightened, human's pace.

Then, a week later, I stopped shaking when I heard a sudden sound.

I found that I was getting better . . . little by little.

It just took time.

A long time.

But the fruit I was hoping for—courage, assurance, confidence in God's goodness—eventually came about.

I'm just glad I didn't give up.

I'm glad I did the work . . . and that I waited.

One last bit of poetry—from the great Robert Frost. His poem, "The Putting in of the Seed," is about a farmer who loves his work . . . and who seems okay with waiting. It ends with the glimmer of hope we're all waiting for:

> How Love burns through the Putting in the Seed
> On through the watching for that early birth
> When, just as the soil tarnishes with weed,
> The sturdy seedling with arched body comes
> Shouldering its way and shedding the earth crumbs.

The seedling will emerge. It will. We just have to wait.

Three Questions

Have you been truly honest with God about any frustrations you have with the waiting part of the growth process?

When is another time in your life when you waited and God ended up giving you what you needed at the right time?

How can you think of your current waiting in terms of smaller time chunks? What's one, reasonable time chunk you can commit to?

Chapter 9
The Harvest

Let us not become weary in doing good, for at the proper time we will reap a harvest if we do not give up.

—Galatians 6:9

The apples have come in. Corn is on the stalks. Roses have blossomed on the bushes. Everything the Farmer has worked for has come to pass. It's time to gather. It's time for the harvest.

The Farmer is thrilled. He laughs as he rushes to collect his bushel buckets and a canvas sack and his thick leather gloves. He knew the seeds would grow into plants that would produce fruit, but that foreknowledge doesn't make the harvest any less joyful.

He climbs up a ladder and plucks a fist-sized red apple off a high branch. He can't help himself—there at the top of the ladder, he polishes the apple on his shirt and takes a bite. The crisp skin gives way to his teeth, and he gets a mouthful of one of the most delicious apples he's ever had. Juice runs down his chin as his mouth curls into a smile. By the time he's down the ladder, he's eaten the entire apple . . . and is about to begin another.

With a bushel basket tucked under one elbow, he walks the rows of corn, carefully picking ears off the tall green stalks. He doesn't just toss the corn into his basket—he lays each ear in, gently and carefully.

He works his clippers on the rose bushes, snipping off long-stemmed red, white, and pink blooms. He lays them in a basket, stacking them up as he goes, creating a simple, beautiful bouquet. The smell is intoxicating.

That night, he enjoys a meal of bread made from wheat he's grown, hot buttered corn fresh from the stalk, a verdant, colorful salad filled with eight different vegetables from his vegetable garden, and a quarter of a rhubarb pie he's baked himself. In the middle of his table, a vase holding fresh-picked carnations, roses, and daisies brings a touch of delicate beauty.

The next day he invites people over. Not just friends—anyone he happens to meet throughout the day. A couple he met at the grocery store. An aimless drifter who hasn't had a vegetable in three months. Even the rude businessman who doubted the Farmer's plan for the land. They all come over. And they eat. And eat. And eat. They eat until they're full and then they eat a little more.

As the meal winds down, the Farmer leans back from the table. He looks around at everyone, eating to their heart's content. He notices how his own pants are a little more snug than they were a few days prior, thanks to all the delicious food. He smiles when he sees their smiles. He knows this is what he's wanted and what they have needed. He's thrilled beyond measure.

His eyes make their way to the window and out toward the land. He looks at it for a long, long moment. He remembers how it was so dry and dusty and full of rocks, stumps, and weeds just months before. He remembers how it looked like the last place in the world that could ever grow food and flowers so delicious and so beautiful. He remembers the work it took. He remembers the waiting it required.

His eyes take in the vegetable garden. And the rose bushes. And the apple trees. And the peach trees. And the quarter mile-wide wheat field.

He looks back at his guests. They're happy and well fed because He knew . . . he knew that little dusty field could be turned into something wonderful.

And this makes the Farmer very happy. Seeing the land bursting with crops, the Farmer believes the field is happy too.

APPRECIATING THE RETURN

There will come a day when you'll notice something different about yourself. A change will have occurred. The good thing you were hoping God was actually growing in you—as you tended and rested and participated and waited—seems to finally be coming to bear.

You have more perseverance than you had six months ago.

You sense you're better at loving your spouse in ways that actually make them feel loved.

You notice a greater tendency to trust God, to believe His love, to rely on His view of you rather than your default view of you.

You discover you don't feel so jealous when something good happens to a friend. Instead, you're naturally happy for them.

You understand what it means to walk in places of authority and responsibility God has given you, and you're actively doing it.

You realize friends are starting to come to you for insight and wisdom.

You're articulating concepts more clearly than you have before. You're finding you can explain and teach truth well.

You're a little more joyful than you used to be.

Or peaceful. Or patient. Or kind or gentle or faithful or in control of yourself or loving.

Now, this may not feel like a full and radical change. You rarely wake up one morning thinking, "Wait. I'm totally different. I'm suddenly completely, fully, totally patient! Yesterday, I yelled at YouTube for taking .07 seconds to load a video, and today I feel like I could stand in line at the DMV for a full two weeks without complaining! Hooray!"

It's usually subtler. You sense it. You feel it. You notice something you hadn't noticed before. Or your friend or spouse points out a change in you.

But it's not so subtle that it's not something real.

You really are a little more patient. Or you can teach better. Or you serve your wife or kids better. Or you lead with a little more confidence.

Fruit is on the vine. A vegetable is on the stalk. Flowers are on the bush. The crops are coming in.

This is the harvest.

A couple weeks ago I had what I'll call a harvest moment. It was a moment when I realized I had stuck with a writing project for four months. It dawned on me I hadn't been counting the days or months—they'd just accumulated as I got up early to write and write and write.

This was new for me. I don't have a long history of staying with projects. I give up at the earliest sign of difficulty or challenge.

And here I was, having logged a lot of hours, having gotten up early and done the work, day after day after day.

I knew it was a harvest because something good had come along. Something good I didn't have in my life before.

I thought, "It worked. All of the tending and waiting has paid off. God's seed turned into something real. God's been faithful to me and to this process, and He's been true to what He said."

And that felt incredible.

And I felt grateful.

And I felt . . . happy.

And though I'm not a dancer (if you saw me dance you'd wonder what strange song in 9/14 time I was hearing in my head), I wanted to do a little dance, right there in my basement.

And I wanted to find out how else I could apply my newfound perseverance.

The harvest was good.

The harvest is good.

It's what, deep down, we've been wanting or needing. It's what will bring good things to our lives and to the lives of the people around us.

So how do we respond to this kind of goodness?

I've found it's good to do five things when the harvest comes in: Be thankful. Celebrate. Remember. Keep going. And share.

THE FARMER WAS RIGHT

True, real, deep gratefulness is better described as praise. Now *praise* is a pretty religious word, but it accurately describes how we're meant to respond to God when something good comes along from Him.

When the harvest comes, it's good for us to praise God to communicate these simple ideas:

1. This crop came because You planted the seed and kept the tending and waiting process going inside of me.
2. You were right all along—good things would come in time, just as You said.
3. I'm glad this crop is here.

How we express these things can happen in a number of different forms.

It may happen when you're at a church service and there's a worship song that points to God, His faithfulness, His love, or how He does good things—even when we're not sure He will. When those kinds of songs come along and I'm in a harvest moment, I love to sing. Something in me feels as though I'm finally singing along in a genuine way—drawing my passion from a legitimate place where I'm truly grateful to God and want to sing out to Him just how good He's been to me. Those times usually choke me up, honestly. My praise tends to get a bit blubbery in harvest seasons.

For me, praise also happens when I'm driving in the car by myself. It could be on the way to Target or to pick up dinner or it could be me driving with the sole purpose of being alone so I can talk to God without anyone else hearing. I tell Him I'm happy He stuck with things when I wanted to give up and that even when I was doing my part—tending and waiting—I realize He gave me the capacity to do all that.

When a harvest comes and I'm not naturally prone to be grateful or to praise, something's wrong. Usually it's because I've believed a lie about how the good that's come isn't really that good or because I've convinced myself the good is really a result of me trying hard.

Me: *Good job, Me!*

Also Me: *Thanks, Me. I couldn't have done it without you, Me.*

Me: *Well, I feel the same way about you, Me.*

Also Me: *We really did it, didn't we?*

Me: *We sure did.*

Also Me: *Isn't it fun to praise ourselves?*

Me: *Eh, not really.*

Also Me: *Yeah, you're right. Sigh.*

Me: *Sigh.*

When we we don't have anyone to thank but ourselves, it leaves us feeling . . . lonely. It can actually become a bit of an existential moment as we lapse into an it's-all-up-to-me-and-whether-I-work-hard philosophy that isolates us from the need for others and, even worse, the entire concept of a God who's friends with us.

(This isn't to say we shouldn't feel proud of the work we've put in to tend the seed and to wait. Clearly we're taking part in the work! It's not ungodly to recognize that. I just know that sometimes I have a tendency to cut God out of the equation altogether, taking full credit for the good that's come.)

When I express gratitude and praise, I affirm to myself that God is really God. Me and my efforts aren't God. Luck isn't God. Other people and what they do for me aren't God. God's God, and I'm happy He's God and not all of those other things—particularly Me.

Earlier I mentioned the talk about gratitude my friend Bob gave. Here are a few of the benefits he cited that scientists had discovered:

⊙ People who feel more gratitude turn out to be more likely to be happy and less likely to be depressed or stressed.

⊙ Gratitude has one of the strongest links with mental health and satisfaction with life of any personality variable.

⊙ Grateful people tend to have better social relationships and contribute more to the harmony of family and community.

I want to be happier and less depressed and stressed! I want to be mentally healthy! I want better relationships! Don't you?

When I get grateful—realizing good comes from somewhere outside myself, somewhere from inside a loving, kind, friendly God—then I get those things. And when I express my respect for Him and His driving of the process, I see myself as provided for and cared for. Something about that always feels right to me. It's comforting.

FANCY FISH AND CHIPS

There's a seafood restaurant near our house that's kinda-sorta fancy. It's got white tablecloths that aren't made out of paper, if that gives you any idea. My wife and I go there once or twice a year.

Typically Kristin gets some crazy fish that's been soaked in wheatgrass juice, grilled, and served on a bed of kale with a side beet-and-cucumber salad. Me? I get something similar: the fully and utterly deep-fried fish and chips with extra tartar sauce.

The fish and chips entrée isn't healthy. It should have a surgeon general's warning on the side of the plate. But, oh man, it's delicious.

Every time we've gone to this place, our waiter begins by welcoming us and asking if we're celebrating any sort of special occasion.

Since we usually only go to this place when we're celebrating, we respond with something like: "Yes! It's our anniversary!" Or, "It's her birthday!" Or, "She just graduated nursing school!"

How weird would it be to say something like, "Well, (reading waiter's name tag), Toby . . . I have had a long-standing problem with giving up on anything that's become challenging or difficult. (Between us, I think it has to do with a fear of failure that crept in because, at a young age, I'd put a lot of expectations on myself, and when I sense a chance of failure, I lose sight of who I really am because my identity is wrapped up in my accomplishments.) Anyway . . . about a year ago, I felt as though God wanted to build perseverance in me. It hasn't been an easy process, Toby. It's been so hard! And the waiting? Oh, man. The waiting was—well, I don't have to tell you. You're a waiter . . . it's right there in your job title. Anyhow, over a long period of time it seems like perseverance is finally coming through in my field—sorry, that's part of a big long metaphor based on 1 Corinthians where Paul says—oh, I won't go into that. But we're both just really glad that God's produced some perseverance in me so . . . I'm gonna have the fish and chips, Toby."

Then Toby would stare at me for a full five seconds without speaking and finally flatly say, "Do you want vinegar with your fish and chips?"

(Telling a waiter you're celebrating an anniversary or birthday is a great way to get a free dessert. Telling him you're celebrating God growing a trait inside you is a great way to get a free cold stare. Not a great way to get free dessert.)

Celebration is something that's sorely lacking in the world of Jesus followers. We don't do it very well. I think it's because we think parties and happy times are (for some reason) not really "God moments."

Our forefathers in the nation of Israel totally got the idea of celebrating. They celebrated all the time! As a matter of fact, there's a type of tithe (ten percent of someone's income) that was explicitly meant to be held aside—get this—so a family could have a big, fun, fancy meal to celebrate God's working in their lives! (Don't believe me? Read Deuteronomy 14:22–27.)

It's important to celebrate wedding anniversaries and birthdays and job promotions. But it's also important to celebrate internal milestones.

Would it be weird to celebrate something like signs of perseverance or a marriage that's finally headed in the right direction or a newly forming gift of evangelism? Maybe. But maybe it would be totally right at the same time.

These celebrations don't have to be huge.

I've celebrated good growing in me by participating in a funny little tradition I've had since college: I stop at a gas station and get a Dr. Pepper and a Twix bar. I drive and enjoy that junk, smiling and thanking God. When I do that, I say, "God, I'm enjoying this DP and Twix because it tastes good to me—just like what You've done in me feels good to me."

Sometimes celebration is just simply sitting with a friend and marveling at what God's done and how far He's taken you—from Point A to Point B.

Why wouldn't we celebrate something like this? As Jesus-followers, don't we think these internal milestones are remarkable? Aren't they worth a few bucks at the fish place or the gas station or some time with a pal considering the good that's come?

Without celebrations, our lives can feel like they're little more than a road trip where we're stuck in the car, never really getting where we think we're going. Celebrations are the times when we stop, get out, look back at the road we've traveled, and appreciate how far we've come.

ROCKS IN A VASE

Imagine a whole nation of people who have been wandering through a desert for forty years. They're exhausted. An entire generation has come and gone. They've been looking for a place to settle down and live. A place where God would give them protection and provision and they could rest.

219

Finally this nation—Israel—is at the doorstep of a wonderful place. They're about to enter the Promised Land.

All that stands between them and their new home is a river.

Do they just rush in and start enjoying what God's given them?

I'm sure they'd like to do that, but instead God has them pause and do something as they head in.

First God stops up the river so the people can cross into the Promised Land on dry earth. (I think one of the reasons God did this was to remind the people how this whole journey started—with God stopping up the Red Sea so those slaves could get free of their Egyptian masters.)

Then as the people walk across, He tells the heads of the twelve main groups of Israelites to each grab one big rock from the bed of the river.

So twelve stones are retrieved.

Next, on the other side of the Jordan River, God tells the Israelites to stack up those stones (probably into a pyramid-type shape, which seems kind of funny and clever considering, again, this nation had been saved from the nation of Egypt, which was not only famous for an alphabet made up of bird shapes and eyes, but for, you know, those pyramids).

God told the Israelites, "Each of you is to take up a stone on his shoulder, according to the number of the tribes of the Israelites, to serve as a sign among you. In the future, when your children ask you, 'What do these stones mean?' tell them that the flow of the Jordan was cut off before the ark of the covenant of the LORD. When it crossed the Jordan, the waters of the Jordan were cut off. These stones are to be a memorial to the people of Israel forever" (Joshua 4:5–7).

Twelve stones, stacked up. Twelve stones that may not have looked like much. Twelves stones serving as a reminder that God is faithful to His promises.

I asked Kristin to marry me on a rocky shore of the Puget Sound. During the proposal I asked her to pick up eleven stones from the ground where we were standing. After she'd chosen the rocks, I got down on one knee and opened a box with a ring inside it and asked her to marry me—telling her the diamond in the ring was the "twelfth stone." (Cheesy as a quesadilla? Sure.)

Kristin and I getting together was, simply put, a miracle of God. No one on earth would have ever put us together. There were all sorts of barriers between us. But God saw fit for her to marry me and me to marry her. And so He did some wild and crazy things to remove those barriers. (Grab me some time and I'll tell you some of our stories over chips and guac.)

We have a big, square vase up on the mantel in our living room. Inside the vase are those eleven stones. They're a symbol of God's faithfulness to us. It's evidence of the fruition of a seed God planted in me long ago about being a husband . . . even though I questioned if that was ever really going to happen throughout much of the waiting.

When our daughters are old enough to ask about the rocks, we'll happily tell them the story of God's faithfulness to bring about what He wanted to bring about despite long odds.

I love having a symbolic, physical reminder of God's goodness. It reminds me that when God plants a seed, it will eventually become something good as we labor and we wait.

Those rocks even encourage us as we go through other challenges. They tell us, "God was faithful to bring about good in your past. Why wouldn't He bring about good in this too?"

"Rocks" don't have to be literal rocks. They can be anything that symbolizes God's goodness to you. Whatever they are, keep them in a place where you see them often so they remind you of the story of God's goodness to you.

How awful would it be to have God grow something good in you but you end up forgetting the journey and trials and the ultimate success He brought about?

Reminders keep that from happening. They help us stay aware that God's good and, sometimes despite barriers and long odds, He brings about wonderful crops.

A BETTER BANANA

Let's say you had a banana plantation, and you've just grown your first crop of bananas. You pull down a bunch from a tree, remove one banana from the bunch, peel it open and take a bite.

You like the banana.

It's kind of firm and almost totally ripe and has a good, though faint, flavor.

It's a pretty good banana.

After celebrating the banana harvest, what would you do? Would you turn to your workers and say, "Well, keep it up. Let's just keep making these bananas, as-is"?

Or would you think about how you got to that banana and consider ways to make an even better banana in the future?

Would you rest with what you have or would you keep going, growing more and better bananas?

When God grows something good inside of us, that's not the end of the story. The crop can always get better.

I have more perseverance than I had six months, a year, two years ago. But I'm not as perseverant as I could be.

I've grown as a husband, but I'm not The Fully Realized, Completely Perfect, Totally Awesome, Servant-Leader Husband I could be.

I've learned to teach and communicate, but I could get better.

The initial fruits are not the final product.

They can't be. They shouldn't be.

Why? Because this is a continual process. God's not a God who grows something and goes, "Eh, good enough." He wants it to get better and sweeter and more refined.

God's constantly helping us grow in the gifts, talents, and abilities He's given us. He's also always helping our spiritual fruit become more pure and more helpful for other people.

There's an element of dissatisfaction that's helpful here. Not a type of dissatisfaction that says, "It's good but not great. Ho-hum," and keeps us from gratitude. It's more of a good type of dissatisfaction that makes us say, "This is great! I'm so grateful for this! And I know it's only going to get better!" It's an excitement that appreciates what God's given and looks forward to how the fruit will grow and mature and become even more of what it's meant to become.

When our girls were born, Kristin and I loved them immediately. They were each perfect to us. But we also knew they'd grow and become more and more of the little girls—and eventually women—they were meant to be. Knowing that didn't make us love them any less when we brought them home from the hospital. ("I guess this one's cute, but she's really not all she's meant to be. I mean, I don't see any talents in her right now except for putting her toes in her mouth. Lame.") No! We appreciated who they were and knew they were going to grow into so much more.

I've been married almost fourteen years. That's fourteen years of God growing me into a better husband. Just this past weekend my wife confronted me with the fact that I'm not good at guiding our family when it comes to spiritual relationships. At first this stung. But after the sting wore off, I realized this was a good (though hard) truth for me to hear. Why? Because it's a new place where God can continue to grow me as a husband. God's shown me a way for my "husband crop" to improve.

My clients become better speakers over time, but if they ever think they're "good enough" they'll always be, well . . . "good enough" speakers, even though they could get better and better.

It's the same with the things God's grown in us. The fruit is good, and it's meant to be better over time.

Good and getting better.

This means we keep going on the journey. We keep finding new ways to be challenged in the areas where God has grown a crop. It means we look forward to better and better versions of the fruit, while being grateful for what we have right now.

GROWN TO BE EATEN

Going back to the Farmer's original vision for the field:

Question: *Why does a farmer grow crops?*

Answer: *To be eaten.*

A farmer doesn't grow corn, admire it, then chunk it into a fire. He doesn't pluck apples so he can see how far he can throw them. Wheat isn't grown so it can just stand there, waving in the wind like one of those twenty-foot-tall, inflatable guys who flop up and down in front of car dealerships.

A few years ago I heard someone teaching about the fruit of the Spirit. I'd heard talks about the fruit of the Spirit all my life. But this teacher said something I'd never heard before. Something simple, but completely profound.

He said, "The fruit of the Spirit is meant to be eaten. It's fruit, after all."

For some reason, I'd never thought of it that way. I'd kind of always thought the fruit of the Spirit was just the quality of character that was nice to have and God wanted us to have and, well, I guess . . . that was all.

But there's a reason God describes those things as fruit. It's fruit because it's meant to be eaten, providing goodness and nourishment for anyone who takes a bite.

So who's eating our crops?

First off, I think God is. That's weird to think, but I believe God is blessed (meaning, He experiences something that's really, really good) when crops grow up in us. Me becoming a more perseverant man? That brings goodness and joy and delight to God. A woman becoming more patient and loving? That brings goodness and joy and delight to God. Someone who exhibits more kindness . . . or a gift of faith . . . or a willingness to be a better friend . . . or bravery . . . or security in God's love? Those all bring goodness and joy and delight to God.

It's hard to stress how big a deal this is, by the way. We can't really see God, so to some degree, we have to imagine this. But can you imagine God delighting and being blessed by something He's grown inside of you? In short, can you picture some character trait growing inside of you actually putting a smile on the face of the God of all creation? It's important to be able to, because if we can't picture things in us bringing pleasure to our Heavenly Daddy, then we're going to feel something lacking in that father/child relationship He wants to have with us.

I'm meant to enjoy the crops that have been grown in my field too.

Enjoying the crop means celebrating and being grateful and being happy that it's come up in my life. But it also means letting my life get a little better because of that crop.

There are so many things in my life I never would've attempted without having the perseverance God's grown in me lately. Writing projects, long-term tasks around the house, us packing up our house and moving—all of those would've been impossible, honestly, without this new perseverance.

I used to give up so easily when resistance came along, wanting to stop the growth of something good. Not so much anymore. I'm currently in a season of waiting for something great to grow within my family. It's taking longer than I'd expected. Way longer. But I'm finding the grace and strength to keep going and not give up because of this newly grown perseverance in me.

Let's say God's grown something in you that makes you a more loving, patient spouse. Now obviously your spouse is going to benefit (more on that in a moment), but *you're* going to benefit from a stronger, happier marriage, right?

When God helps me become a better father, I like spending time with my daughters even more—and that father/daughter relationship brings even more joy to my life.

When I forgive, I take a step toward possibly getting back an old relationship I was missing.

When God grows the ability to rest in me, I get rid of stress and worry and anxiety and find myself able to know what's my responsibility and what is God's.

When I'm selfless, I don't sense I'm ruled by the tyranny of self, which demands I be the center of all of my decision-making. I can ease up and not let pleasure rule my life. And that feels freeing.

When God's grown security in me, I don't feel so fragile. I can enter situations with confidence, knowing my worth isn't tied up in what I do or how I do it. Instead, I'm at peace because my worth is tied up in Him and His love for me.

My life gets better when I get to partake in the crops God's grown in me.

But the benefits of the good things God grows in us aren't limited to those experienced by God and by us. We were meant to share our crops with others so they can eat them and enjoy the benefits of them too.

THE CONFIDENT ORANGE PROVIDER

Imagine you're walking along a street and you meet someone standing beside a wheelbarrow full of oranges. Bright, clean, juicy oranges. There must be two dozen of them.

"What are you doing with all of those oranges?" you ask.

"Eh, not sure. Just ate one. It was good," the Orange Guy says.

"Oh. Okay. Well, they sure look good," you say.

"Oh, yeah," the Orange Guy says. "They are."

You shrug your shoulders and are about to ask more about the oranges when you notice a guy, not ten feet from the Orange Guy, who's coughing.

"You okay, man?" you ask the Coughing Guy.

"Yeah, I—" he coughs four more times—"just can't seem to get over this"—coughs again—"cold. Had it forever."

"You know what you need? Some vitamin C," you say.

The Coughing Guy coughs again then says, "Yeah, probably."

You look back at the Orange Guy, standing there with all those oranges—each one full of about a billion milligrams of vitamin C.

Then you look back to the Coughing Guy who's still coughing.

And you stand there thinking, "Now, why won't Orange Guy give Coughing Guy an orange? He's got plenty. They look amazing. Clearly Coughing Guy needs an orange or two, right?"

So, you go up to Orange Guy and say, "Hey, buddy. You know, that guy over there could really use one of your oranges. That vitamin C could really help him out."

The Orange Guy looks over at the Coughing Guy and says, "Yeah, I thought I heard some coughing. Boy, that guy looks rough." Then the Orange Guy goes back to what he was doing: staring into space.

"But," you say, "don't you want to give an orange to Coughing Guy? You know, to help him out?"

The Orange Guy screws up his face in confusion. "What do you want me to do? You want me to give an orange to him?"

"Yes! You'll never eat all of those—"

"He doesn't want an orange. I mean, I don't really even have oranges."

You look at the Orange Guy's giant pile of oranges and you say, "Uhhh . . . yes you do. See all those orange fruit things? Those are oranges."

"Well," the Orange Guy says, "they're not any good."

"Are you kidding? Those look like great oranges."

"Well . . ." the Orange Guy pauses and thinks. Then says, "I'd seem like a jerk if I went up to him and said, 'Hey, man. I have an orange for you.'"

"A jerk? You think that would make you seem like a jerk?"

"Yeah. He'd be all like, 'Oh, I guess you think you're so important with your oranges and that I can't quit coughing without your oranges so here's an orange, man.' He'd think I was arrogant."

You're stunned. "I do not see how he would think you're arrogant."

"He just would," Orange Guy says.

You walk up to Coughing Guy and, after you wait for a break in his coughing, you say, "Would you think Orange Guy was a jerk if he gave you an orange?"

Coughing Guy thinks, then says, "No. I'd just eat the orange to get the vitamin C I need, and then I'd thank him."

You go back to Orange Guy and tell him what Coughing Guy said.

Orange Guy thinks about it and then says, "Nah. He'd probably think I was a jerk."

You shake your head looking at Orange Guy and all of his oranges and at Coughing Guy with his vitamin C deficiency, not ten steps away.

Sharing the good things God's grown in us requires objectivity. Objectivity is the ability to consider yourself in a way that doesn't take into account that you're considering yourself. In other words, you think about you and what you have to offer with the same non-bias as though you were talking about someone else.

If I'm truly objective, there will be times when I realize something God has grown in me is good to share with someone else. Say God's given me the ability to explain complex or abstract ideas in clear, understandable ways. Well, if I'm objective, when I run into someone who needs a complex or abstract idea explained in a clear, understandable way, I'll think, "Hey! I know someone who can communicate complex or abstract ideas in a clear, understandable way: me!" and then I go about doing what I can to help the person by communicating the complex or abstract idea in a clear, understandable way. (The trick is helping with kindness, empathy, and grace. No one wants to receive anything from an arrogant or condescending person.)

Hoosiers is a fantastic sports movie. It's about a small town high school basketball team in Indiana who—through grit, hard work, and determination—make it to the state championship game against all odds.

In the last moments of the movie—in the final seconds of the game—the team ties the game up. The coach (played by Gene Hackman) calls time out. He gathers the team in a huddle to call the final play of the game.

He looks around at the team and points to Jimmy, a quiet, shy, reserved player—who's also an incredible, lights-out, pure shooter. He's meek as a lamb, but when he shoots, he consistently puts the ball in the basket.

Jimmy's character flaw throughout the movie, though, has been a lack of confidence. Yes, he's the best shooter, but he doesn't see himself that way.

In this final, high-pressure moment, the coach doesn't draw up a play with Jimmy shooting the final shot. Instead, he says the other team may be expecting Jimmy to take the shot, so they're going to give it to another player to shoot.

The team's collective faces fall. They're clearly disappointed.

Coach: "What's the matter with you guys?"

No one says anything. Then, angrily, Coach asks again, "What's the matter with you?!"

The team's disappointed Jimmy isn't taking the shot. They know he's good. They know he's their best hope.

And then the camera shows us Jimmy. For the first time, we see quiet, reserved, shy Jimmy realize he's the team's best hope too.

He's become objectively and humbly confident he's the right guy.

In his small, quiet voice, Jimmy says simply, "I'll make it."

Jimmy is stepping up. Jimmy is seeing himself like his teammates see him. Jimmy knows he's the right guy to shoot the ball.

And suddenly Coach sees that not only could Jimmy hit this shot, but he can hit it in this moment. Jimmy is the guy.

Coach changes the play. The ball's gonna go to Jimmy. Jimmy's going to shoot.

And what happens?

Jimmy gets the ball.

Jimmy shoots.

Jimmy makes the winning shot.

And Hickory High wins the state championship.

This wouldn't have happened if Jimmy saw himself subjectively—going with how he felt about himself. It wouldn't have happened if Jimmy had doubted the talent he had. It wouldn't have happened if Jimmy had worried how his team would've felt about him making the shot.

It's common for us to experience a natural push back that says the good thing God has grown in us isn't really that good, isn't wanted by others, or we will be perceived of as an arrogant jerk when offered.

Lots of Jesus followers have a strong gag reflex toward arrogance (and rightly so), yet this can lead to something on the other end of the spectrum that's just as bad as arrogance: false humility.

False humility says, "Oh, no. Not me. Not what I have. They don't want it. It's not that good. They won't like me if I offer it."

Imagine Superman standing on a street in Metropolis watching a guy falling from the top of a skyscraper and saying to himself, "Wow. Somebody should really help that guy." That's false humility.

But just as God never wanted us to grow into arrogant jerks who think we're the saviors of the world, He also doesn't want us short-selling what He's grown inside of us.

It's hard to wrap our minds around this, but when we short-sell those things, we're not being humble—we're actually insulting the work God has done.

And insulting God isn't cool.

Instead of steering away from opportunities, we need to steer ourselves toward opportunities to share the good stuff God's grown inside of us.

My life is markedly different because other people have offered up the crops God has grown within them to me. By eating that fruit, my life has had more of a tendency to head in the direction it's meant to be headed.

I've said before that God has made my wife an encourager. She sees people getting down and frustrated as they try and fail, and something inside of her leaps up, causing her to tell the person not to give up, to keep going, and to be hopeful.

She was just encouraging me this morning, reminding me there's an end to a very chaotic season we're in right now. She calmed me down and gave me hope. Without the encouragement of my wife, I know I'd be prone to live the life of Eeyore, grumpy and frustrated, and continually giving up.

My pal Steven has faith like you wouldn't believe. This guy just plain believes. His extreme faith in God and God's ultimate goodness and power is so radical it can be off-putting to some. But to me it acts as a reminder that God's not some otherworldly guy who can do kind-of amazing things like impressive card tricks or the thing where it looks like your finger is coming apart. He's God. He can do anything. And He's going to do everything He's said He will do. I like when

Steven shares the faith he has with me. If he didn't, I'd be more prone to think of God as less-than—a deity I can't fully trust.

My dad loves to serve people. This is something God has grown in my father over a long period of time. What makes him happiest is jumping up and doing something for someone else. He loves to help others. When he sees someone in need— someone who can't figure something out themselves or needs a hand doing whatever they're doing—Dad dives in. It could be helping them put in an A/C unit, running to the store to pick up some ice cream, or just being a steady workhorse who brings home a paycheck—my dad serves.

When my dad serves me, I know how much he loves me. I feel cared for—even at my age—and thought about and watched over.

Not only that, but how my dad serves me has given me insight into how God serves us. The engine inside Jesus that had Him washing His friends' feet the night before He died is the same engine at work inside my dad. I see God better through how my dad serves me.

Late in life my mom allowed God to wake up a long dormant gift for teaching inside her. She started sharing truths from the Bible with people, helping them grasp some of what God's been doing in the world and what He continues to do. Now, fifteen years later, someone who's at the age when she could be "taking it easy" regularly speaks to a group of 150 or so who count on her to clearly (with warmth, humor, and fantastic metaphors and storytelling) articulate God's truths.

What if my wife didn't encourage me? What if Steven didn't talk to me about his faith and how he was seeing God? What if my father never went out of his way to serve me and help me? What if my mother never taught people about God in the way only she can?

And what if the authors I love to read, who help me gain a deeper understanding of God, had never offered to me—and the public—that crop of clear communication? What if the good bosses I've had never leveraged their understanding of authority and how to lead well? What if my friends kept their patience and forgiveness crops to themselves?

I can't imagine how my life would be if the people around me either felt too unconfident to share the good things God had grown in them with me . . . or just didn't care to share them . . . or questioned whether or not that fruit was really in their field.

Sharing fruit with others really comes down to one motivating factor: love.

> If I speak in the tongues of men or of angels, but do not have love, I am only a resounding gong or a clanging cymbal. If I have the gift of prophecy and can fathom all mysteries and all knowledge, and if I have a faith that can move mountains, but do not have love, I am nothing. If I give all I possess to the poor and give over my body to hardship that I may boast, but do not have love, I gain nothing.
>
> —1 Corinthians 13:1–3

Paul calls for us Jesus followers to help each other by sharing the good things God has grown in us (giving insights into how God sees things, sharing wisdom, giving generously), but he warns us that if we do those things without loving the people we're sharing with, then it all comes up short.

He's really talking about our motives. Why do we do what we do? Why do we do good things? Is it because we love people . . . or is it because we're trying to gain something for ourselves?

Doing something good to feel better about ourselves or earn a better reputation or score imaginary brownie points with God won't produce lasting results or provide us with the motivation we need to become people who consistently share good things.

Love is the only motivator that will do that.

What if the Orange Guy loved Coughing Guy? What if he really and truly cared about him? Wouldn't that love override any form of consideration of his own pride? Wouldn't he rush to bring an orange—or a whole bushel of oranges—to Coughing Guy?

What if he didn't even know Coughing Guy? Could he still have such love in his heart toward *all* people that when he saw someone in need of an orange, he'd run as fast as his feet could carry him to bring what was needed?

Love moves us. It leads us. It motivates us.

It causes us to share the good things God's grown inside of us with other people.

It doesn't lead us to hoard or let pride keep us from taking a risk in sharing.

Love is what motivated God to share the good things He has with us in the first place. "For God so loved the world that he gave his one and only Son" (John 3:16).

Through love, I can be like God. I can be useful. I can help. I can provide. I can give.

Just like Jesus did.

When we live like this and the people around us live like this, the world becomes more like the world God wants our world to become. It begins with you. And it begins with me. It begins with all of us believing we have what God says we have and then letting love motivate us to share it with others.

Then people get what they deeply need. And then they're able to grow into people who have things other people need. And the sharing and the receiving goes on and on and on.

That's a beautiful world, isn't it?

C. S. Lewis said it this way: "The more we thus share the Heavenly Bread between us, the more we shall all have."

Amen to that, huh?

Amen to this too:

> Land that drinks in the rain often falling on it and that produces a crop useful to those for whom it is farmed receives the blessing of God.
>
> —Hebrews 6:7

Three Questions

How do you like communicating gratitude to God the most?

How can you celebrate something good God's grown inside you?

Being motivated by love, what's one way you could share a good crop God's grown in you with someone else?

Chapter 10
The Kingdom

The kingdom of God is in your midst.

—Luke 17:21

The Farmer walks.

He walks across the field, once again admiring all that's been grown on the land.

But he walks even further.

He walks onto another field.

Here he sees crops he's helped grow on that land. Crops that are different from the ones on the first field.

And he walks even further.

He walks onto another field and sees an entirely different collection of crops. And some boulders and weeds that still need removal.

And he walks even further.

He walks across field after field, taking in the uniqueness of each field—how each have their own crops and each are in their own state of preparation, waiting, and growth.

Field after field after field.

They're all separate and distinct . . .

And yet somehow they're all connected.

If one field is in disrepair, that somehow keeps the fields near it from growing all the crops it could be growing.

But if one field flourishes, the adjacent ones are more likely to flourish as well.

As the Farmer walks, it's clear the earth is full of fields.

He loves each and every field.

He wants the best for each field.

And as each field's potential becomes more and more realized, the entire earth starts to become more and more of what it's meant to become.

When Jesus walked around on earth, talking with his friends and teaching them about God and what God wanted for the world, He continually brought up the kingdom of heaven (sometimes referring to it as the kingdom of God).

He told them there are two kingdoms in the world: the kingdom where people recognize God as King and the kingdom where God isn't recognized as King. Jesus, being a big fan of God's, always promoted the one where God is recognized as King.

In that kingdom—the kingdom of heaven—things are good. In the kingdom of heaven, those in need have their needs looked after. The lonely are given friendship. The beaten down are lifted up. The scoundrels are given forgiveness. The confused are given direction. The hopeless are given hope. The faithless find faith. The sick are healed. The exhausted are given rest. The unloved finally feel love.

Jesus identified places in the world where the kingdom of heaven was advancing and growing. He affirmed those places, pointed them out to His buddies, and said, "Look at this! Isn't this fantastic? This is just what God, the King, wants!" Jesus loves the kingdom of heaven because, in those places, God's heart is most purely expressed to humans. When the needy have their needs met, they realize God is a caring God. When the lonely are given friendship, they realize God is relational. When the faithless find faith, they realize God can be trusted. When the unloved feel love, they realize that—quite simply— God is love.

Jesus' hope for His friends—and all His followers who would come along in the centuries after—was they would live in the kingdom of heaven while down here on earth. To Jesus, this means two things: 1.) His followers will receive the good, great, amazing things living in the kingdom of heaven would give them and 2.) His followers will take part in the kingdom of heaven, helping give to others the wonderful things God wants them to have.

Again, two parts to the kingdom of heaven: receiving and giving.

To get a better grasp of where all this about fields and crops and farmers and growth is meant to ultimately lead us, let's adjust our metaphor a bit.

Instead of thinking of yourself as the field, think of yourself as the landowner of the field. You're the one who's allowed the Farmer to come along and care for the field, growing good things on it.

Now imagine yourself—a landowner—walking along the land, taking a look at all of the good things that have grown on the land. You see the cotton and the roses and the potatoes and the corn and the wheat and the apples. You stop by a bush dotted with bright red strawberries. You kneel down, pluck one off, and pop it in your mouth. It's wonderfully sweet and wholly refreshing. You smell a magnolia blossom, letting the aroma fill your nose and lungs. You taste a carrot. You chew on a sprig of mint.

Then you notice someone walking past your land. This person looks like they could use a strawberry. So you give them one. Then a few more. They're happy and thankful.

A few moments later, someone else walks past. She's looking for something. You ask what she's looking for. "Corn," she says. This makes you smile because you have a bushel sitting right at your feet. You give it to her.

Still another person passes. At first they refuse your offer of a carrot, but they eventually accept. "This is a fantastic carrot," they say. And then they eat another.

This sharing makes you happy.

Then you notice something you hadn't noticed before. You notice other fields beyond your own field. Some of them are well cared for, and others are in serious disrepair. You also notice each of these fields has a landowner standing on it. One is the person you gave the strawberries to, one is the one looking for corn, another is the person who appreciated your carrots. Other fields beyond those have other landowners.

On one field, you see a line of trees that are shorter and a little thinner than apple trees. You walk across your field to the edge of it so you can get a better look. Only then do you notice the trees are peach trees.

Those peaches look really good to you. You don't have any peaches on your field, and you can't remember the last time you had a good peach.

The landowner notices you admiring the peaches.

"Would you like one?"

"Yes, please," you say.

He plucks a peach off the tree and hands it to you. You take a bite. It's fantastic. Juicy, sweet, soft, but firm.

Moments later, the person you shared corn with passes by. She eyes the peaches too. She's offered one. She eats it. And loves it.

Another landowner tells the others about the lettuce that's growing on her field. "You're more than welcome to some," she says.

Over time, the other landowners and you are sharing and receiving from each other all the time. Not only that, but each landowner is further inspired to grow more and more crops and to give them away more and more confidently.

Soon everyone in the area is getting what they need while giving away what they have.

Not only that, but one day one landowner decides to gather a bunch of the lettuce she's grown on her land and get on a plane to travel to a faraway land to hand out some of her lettuce.

That person in the faraway land gets what they need. Then, in turn, they discover what they need to grow crops on their own land. And then they share with the people around them. Then those people grow good things on their fields.

Your field no longer feels like a lonely, solitary field. It's a field that's next to other fields. And you're no longer a lonely, solitary landowner. You're surrounded by other landowners. And you no longer grow things just for you. You share them with others. And you no longer only eat what you have grown on your field. You receive from others, getting so much more of what you need.

In the midst of it all, the Farmer watches. He's the one who oversees the growth on all the fields. He ensures the right things are growing at the right time in the right way so everyone gets the crops they truly need.

He sees each field become the field it was destined to become.

It makes him proud . . . and it brings Him joy.

This is what I want for my life: becoming what God wants me to become, giving good things to others, and receiving good things from them.

I want to trust Him because I believe He's completely wise and totally loving.

I want Him to be proud of what's going on in my life. I want it to bring God joy. I want to come alive because of what He's doing in me.

I want good things growing up in me. I want that for you too. God does too.

He wants to come alongside you and show love to you.

He wants to live out a personal and intimate friendship with you.

He wants to convince you He's absolutely trustworthy— completely wise and totally loving.

He wants to gently remove those things in your life that aren't good for you and aren't helpful in bringing about the good He wants to produce in you.

He wants to communicate His words to you—the things He's thinking about you and your incredible potential.

He wants to help you fight lies and resistance so His words can do their good work in you.

He wants to teach you to take both small and large steps that together allow the good things He's wanting to produce in you to grow and grow and grow.

He wants to rest with you and hope with you and wait with you in times when it seems as though nothing is happening.

And He wants to celebrate with you when good things finally emerge in your life, throwing His arms around you and laughing and rejoicing as both you and the world around you benefit from the blessing that's come through all that's been grown in you.

Why does He do all of this?

Because He is the Farmer—and you are a field.

Acknowledgments

Bob Klitgaard—if you hadn't started me on this journey—and checked in to pilot and encourage along the way—I would've lacked the courage and direction needed to write this book.

Whitney Prosperi—your persistence, generosity, and eagerness are why these words have seen the light of day.

Iron Stream Media—particularly Ramona, Tina, Reagan, Meredith, John, and everyone else who lent a hand—you took something that lived on my computer and turned it into an actual book.

Mike Yeager—your creative eye, input, and support have been invaluable.

Ben Hart—your early design contributions helped me see the book differently.

Jay Pickard—you swung in with your expertise at just the right moment.

Tory Leggat—your ceaseless excitement, enthusiasm, and championing provided momentum just when it was needed. See you next quarter.

Steven Manuel, Jeeva Ratnathicam, Andrew Brumme, Keenan Barber, the Masters—you've all had such a profound influence on me and how I see God that your fingerprints are on each page.

Everybody who has let me try to explain God to them—especially the University Ministries students, North attendees, Room adventurers, kids and staff at YSSC, and Restoration folks—your listening ears, grace, feedback, and affirmations have kept me going and growing.

Early manuscript readers—you answered the call, read my sloppy drafts, gave me invaluable feedback, and (more than anything) encouraged me. You'll never know how much that encouragement means to me.

The people I've never met but who taught me about grace and the immense love of Abba Father—including Louie Giglio back in the Choice Ministries days, Wayne Jacobsen, and (most of all) Brennan Manning—you each helped free this guy from dead religion so he could live out a love relationship with Jesus. Now the good news is really good news to me.

If you enjoyed this book, will you consider sharing the message with others?

Let us know your thoughts at info@ironstreammedia.com. You can also let the author know by visiting or sharing a photo of the cover on our social media pages or leaving a review at a retailer's site. All of it helps us get the message out!

Facebook.com/IronStreamMedia

Iron Stream Books is an imprint of Iron Stream Media, which derives its name from Proverbs 27:17, "As iron sharpens iron, so one person sharpens another."

This sharpening describes the process of discipleship, one to another. With this in mind, Iron Stream Media provides a variety of solutions for churches, missionaries, and nonprofits ranging from in-depth Bible study curriculum and Christian book publishing to custom publishing and consultative services. Through our popular Life Bible Study, Student Life Bible Study brands, and New Hope imprints, ISM provides web-based full-year and short-term Bible study teaching plans as well as printed devotionals, Bibles, and discipleship curriculum.

For more information on ISM and Iron Stream Books, please visit

IronStreamMedia.com

THE
RESTORED
MAN

GOD IS THE ULTIMATE RESTORATION EXPERT

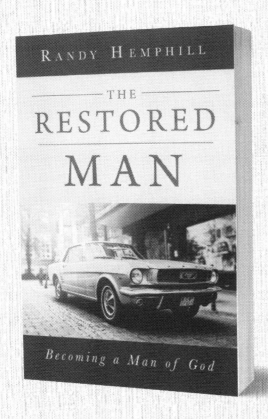

RITE of PASSAGE

The Making of a Godly Man

RITE of

The Maki

ERIC BALLAR

Available from NewHopePublishers.com
and your favorite retailer.

Printed in the United States
By Bookmasters